"ANSWERING THE CALL OF THOSE IN NEED"

A Telephone Pioneers of America Nutritional Cookbook

Telephone Pioneers of America

ANSWERING THE CALL OF THOSE IN NEED

ANSWERING THE CALL OF THOSE IN NEED

Alene White, Chapter Pioneer Administrator
Linda G. Anderson, Chapter Cookbook Chairperson

Cover photography by: Llew Chapman
Design by: Glenda Buchanan, Green Hills Council

This book is a collection of our favorite recipes
which are not necessarily original recipes.

Published by: Favorite Recipes® Press
P.O. Box 305142
Nashville, Tennessee 37230

Manufactured in the United States of America
First Printing: 1991, 30,000 copies

Library of Congress Number: 91-7469
ISBN: 0-87197-297-2

PIONEERING

The Association, named Telephone Pioneers of America, was founded in 1911 when the telephone was only 35 years old.

The Telephone Pioneers of America is the world's largest industry-related volunteer organization in the world. Comprising more than 800,000 members including both active and retired employees of the telecommunications industry, the members contribute more than 25 million volunteer hours a year in Community Service.

Tennessee Pioneers have been major contributors to Children's Hospitals, Special Olympics, Juvenile Diabetes and the March of Dimes. As an 80-year-old organization, the Telephone Pioneers today focus their efforts in a wide range of causes: illiteracy, drug abuse, environmental and hearing impaired to name a few.

With the purchase of this cookbook you will have helped us to continue our Community Service work.

We thank you for your interest.

Alene E. White

Alene E. White
Pioneer Administrator
Tennessee Chapter #21

Telephone Pioneers of America
Councils of Tennessee Chapter #21

Andrew Jackson	Jackson
Chattanooga	Knoxville West
Clarksville	Memphis
Columbia	Nashboro
Green Hills	Suburban East
Harpeth	

IN APPRECIATION

Our previous cookbooks, *Dining With Pioneers I* and *Dining With Pioneers II*, have been a tremendous success. More recently, *Just KID-DING Around*, our young people's cookbook, has proven to be a success with thousands of young cooks.

We are now pleased to introduce this cookbook, *Answering the Call of Those in Need* which is a master collection of **nutritional** recipes.

Thanks to all who have contributed recipes for this cookbook. A special thanks to Tennessee Chapter #21's Cookbook Chairperson, Linda Anderson, whose hard work and effort, has made *Answering the Call of Those in Need* a reality.

Gary Buchanan

Gary Buchanan
President
Tennessee Chapter #21

SPECIAL ACKNOWLEDGEMENTS

The Tennessee Telephone Pioneers of America are grateful for the continued support and efforts of the many individuals who helped in the production of this cookbook. The Pioneers would especially like to recognize the following contributors:

Diana Adcock
Linda G. Anderson
Diane H. Arnold
Teresa Beasley
Paul E. Bridges
Glenda Buchanan
David Bursey
Peggy M. Camp
Sandy Carney
Christina Childress
Katheren Schilling Chinn
Barbara Coulter
Betty Cox
Janice Cude
Jackie Dandridge
Delight W. Everett
Wilma Fletcher
Carol Gilliland
Cherie Greenway
Patricia A. Hanna
Karen S. Hodge
Nina Holmes
Mary Ising

Melissa Elaine Johnson
Zennie Johnson
Ida Jane Love
Nancy Massengill
Cora Y. May
Sarah Beth Miller
Jeannie Patton
Mary M. Pendergrass
Mary Ann Pierce
Joy M. Pursley
Marilyn Putnam
Shirley Robertson
Nancy Rosdeutscher
Nancy C. Stansell
Patsy E. Stow
Ilagene Tribble
Cynthia P. Vance
Marva A. Wade
Doris G. Weakley
Norma K. Webb
Della M. Welch
Alene E. White

NUTRITION AND YOU

People have begun to think of food as something other than a way to fill a hungry stomach or a requirement at social occasions. Until now, cookbooks have told us how to cook but not what to cook or why. For the first time in history the important thing about food is not the way it tastes but what it can do to improve the body. Yes, improve — not just maintain. Some of the changes you can make have been shown to reduce your chances of heart problems, cancer and diabetes. Obviously, a life-long healthy diet is the best, but it is never too late.

The key to smart eating is knowledge. This book will furnish you with some of what you want to know to eat smart, which does not mean eating dull unsatisfying food. It will require making some changes in your present diet, but meat eaters need not become vegetarians, and desserts are still on the menu.

Current thinking targets Fat, Cholesterol and Sodium as prime health problems. All three can be significantly reduced in our diets while retaining flavor and variety that satisfy. Each requires that we be aware of the problem, careful in selecting and preparing our food and, most important, committed to making a change in lifestyle.

Everything you eat supplies calories to give the body energy. The trick is in selecting foods that give you energy and more — protein to build, repair and renew body tissues; vitamins and minerals to help in complex body functions; fiber (both soluble and insoluble) for bulk; fat (unsaturated in small amounts) to dissolve fat-soluble vitamins.

Some of the choices you should make depend on knowing what to avoid or reduce while keeping or increasing those essentials that promote health.

While most of us are able to manipulate our diets with ease, there are those who really need the advice of a Registered Dietitian. If you have hypertriglyceridemia, diabetes, phenylketonuria (PKU) or other diseases that require close monitoring, please consult a specialist before attempting any dietary changes.

CONTENTS

Nutritional Analysis Guidelines 8

Appetizers and Beverages 9

Salads 25

Meats and Meatless Main Dishes 51

Poultry and Seafood 83

Vegetables and Side Dishes 121

Breads 141

Desserts 153

Special Helps 169
   Herbs and Spices 170
   The Well-Balanced Diet 171
   Dietary Exchanges 172
   Selecting the Best Foods 174
   Healthy Shopping 176
   Dietary Fiber in Foods 180
   No-Salt Seasoning 182

Index 183

Order Information 189

NUTRITIONAL ANALYSIS GUIDELINES

The editors have attempted to present these family recipes in a form that allows approximate nutritional values to be computed. Persons with dietary or health problems or whose diets require close monitoring should not rely solely on the nutritional information provided. They should consult their physicians or a registered dietitian for specific information.

Abbreviations for Nutritional Analysis

Cal — Calories
Prot — Protein
Carbo — Carbohydrates

Fiber — Dietary Fiber
T Fat — Total Fat
Chol — Cholesterol

Sod — Sodium
gr — gram
mg — milligrams

Nutritional information for these recipes is computed from information derived from many sources, including materials supplied by the United States Department of Agriculture, computer databanks and journals in which the information is assumed to be in the public domain. However, many specialty items, new products and processed foods may not be available from these sources or may vary from the average values used in these analyses. More information on new and/or specific products may be obtained by reading the nutrient labels. Unless otherwise specified, the nutritional analysis of these recipes is based on level measurements and the following standards.

- **Artificial sweeteners** vary in use and strength so should be used "to taste," using the recipe ingredients as a guideline.
- **Artificial sweeteners** using aspertame (NutraSweet and Equal) should not be used as a sweetener in recipes involving prolonged heating which reduces the sweet taste. For further information on the use of these sweeteners, refer to package information.
- **Alcoholic ingredients** have been analyzed for the basic ingredients, although cooking causes the evaporation of alcohol thus decreasing the caloric content.
- **Buttermilk**, **sour cream** and **yogurt** are the types available commercially.
- **Cake mixes** prepared according to package directions include 3 eggs and ½ cup oil.
- **Chicken,** cooked for boning and chopping, has been roasted; this method yields the lowest caloric values.
- **Cottage cheese** is cream-style with 4.2% creaming mixture. Dry-curd cottage cheese has no creaming mixture.
- **Eggs** are all large.
- **Flour** is unsifted all-purpose flour.
- **Garnishes**, serving suggestions and other optional additions and variations are not included in the analysis.
- **Margarine** and **butter** are regular, not whipped or presoftened.
- **Milk** is whole milk, 3.5% butterfat. Lowfat milk is 1% butterfat. Evaporated milk is whole milk with 60% of the water removed.
- **Oil** is any type of vegetable oil. **Shortening** is hydrogenated vegetable shortening.
- **Salt** and other ingredients to taste have not been included in the analysis.
- If an ingredient shows a variable amount, the analysis reflects the larger.
- **Dietary exchanges** are calculated based on the 1986 American Diabetes Association exchange system. Recipes containing more than 1 teaspoon sugar per serving are not recommended for persons with diabetes.

Appetizers
and Beverages

ALL NATURAL
APPLE CIDER

MEXICAN DUNK

4 medium tomatoes, chopped
2 bunches green onions, chopped
1 6-ounce can sliced black olives, drained

2 4-ounce cans chopped green chilies
Chopped garlic to taste
2 teaspoons olive oil
2 teaspoons vinegar

Combine tomatoes and green onions in serving bowl. Add olives and green chilies; mix well. Add garlic, olive oil and vinegar; mix well. Chill, covered, until serving time. Serve with tortillas. May serve over avocado and top with shredded cheese as salad; may serve over baked potato, or on grilled or poached fish.
Yield: 16 servings.

Approx Per Serving: Cal 33; Prot 1 g; Carbo 3 g; Fiber 1 g;
    T Fat 3 g; Chol 0 mg; Sod 278 mg.

Dietary Exchanges: Vegetable 1/2; Fat 1/2

PICANTE SAUCE

1 15-ounce can whole tomatoes
1 tablespoon olive oil
1 tablespoon vinegar

1 small jalapeño pepper, seeded, sliced
Salt to taste

Mash tomatoes with spoon in saucepan. Stir in olive oil, vinegar, jalapeño pepper and salt. Cook over medium heat for 10 minutes. Chill, covered, until serving time. Serve with tortilla chips. May serve hot over poached fish. May substitute 1/2 teaspoon crushed red pepper for jalapeño pepper. Yield: 8 servings.

Approx Per Serving: Cal 27; Prot 1 g; Carbo 3 g; Fiber <1 g;
    T Fat 2 g; Chol 0 mg; Sod 87 mg.

Dietary Exchanges: Vegetable 1/2; Fat 1/2

PINEAPPLE CHEESE BALL

¼ **cup chopped green bell pepper**
¼ **cup shredded carrot**
1 **8-ounce can juice-pack crushed pineapple, drained**
8 **ounces Neufchâtel cheese, softened**
½ **cup unsalted sunflower seed**

Combine green pepper, carrot, pineapple and Neufchâtel cheese in bowl; mix well. Chill, covered, for 1 hour or until firm. Shape into ball on waxed paper. Roll in sunflower seed, coating well. Chill, covered, until serving time. Place on serving plate. Serve with wheat crackers or Melba toast rounds. Yield: 48 tablespoons.

Approx Per Tablespoon: Cal 24; Prot 1 g; Carbo 1 g; Fiber <1 g;
    T Fat 2 g; Chol 4 mg; Sod 19 mg.

Dietary Exchanges: Fat ½

RELISH DIP

2 **4-ounce cans chopped green chilies**
4 **ounces green salad olives, chopped**
4 **green onions, chopped**
3 **tomatoes, chopped**
2 **tablespoons wine vinegar**
1 **tablespoon oil**
2 **jalapeño peppers, chopped**
Salt and pepper to taste

Combine green chilies, olives, green onions, tomatoes, vinegar, oil and jalapeño peppers in bowl; mix well. Add salt and pepper. Chill until serving time. Serve with tortilla chips. Yield: 12 servings.

Approx Per Serving: Cal 32; Prot <1 g; Carbo 3 g; Fiber <1 g;
    T Fat 2 g; Chol 0 mg; Sod 470 mg.

Dietary Exchanges: Vegetable ½; Fat ½

☎ Make **Mock Sour Cream** by processing ⅔ cup low-fat cottage cheese, ¼ cup water and 1 teaspoon lemon juice in blender until smooth.

AVOCADO AND SALMON SPREAD

1 large avocado, mashed
1 8-ounce can salmon,
  drained, mashed
1/2 cup ricotta cheese
1/4 cup thinly sliced green
  onions
1 green bell pepper, finely
  chopped

2 teaspoons prepared
  mustard
1 teaspoon prepared
  horseradish
1/8 teaspoon lemon pepper
Garlic powder to taste

Combine avocado, salmon and ricotta cheese in bowl; mix well. Add green onions, green pepper, mustard, horseradish, lemon pepper and garlic powder; mix well. Spoon into serving bowl. Garnish with alfalfa sprouts. Serve with assorted crackers.
Yield: 48 tablespoons.

Approx Per Tablespoon: Cal 18; Prot 1 g; Carbo <1 g; Fiber <1 g;
    T Fat 1 g; Chol 1 mg; Sod 33 mg.

Dietary Exchanges: Free

BEEFY CHEESE SPREAD

8 ounces light cream cheese,
  softened
1 8-ounce can crushed
  pineapple, drained

1 2 1/2-ounce package dried
  beef, chopped
1/3 cup chopped chives

Combine cream cheese and pineapple in bowl; mix well. Add dried beef and chives; mix well. Chill until serving time. Serve with crackers. Yield: 42 tablespoons.

Approx Per Tablespoon: Cal 20; Prot 1 g; Carbo 1 g; Fiber <1 g;
    T Fat 1 g; Chol 20 mg; Sod 80 mg.

Dietary Exchanges: Free

☎ Make a delicious healthy **Base for Dips** by processing equal parts of yogurt and low-fat ricotta cheese in a blender until smooth and the consistency of sour cream. Use as sour cream substitute in your favorite recipes.

MELON BASKET

1 small oval watermelon
2 cups cantaloupe balls
2 cups honeydew melon balls
2 cups fresh pineapple
   chunks

2 cups fresh strawberries or
   raspberries
1 cup plain low-fat yogurt
2 tablespoons lemon juice
1/2 teaspoon poppy seed

Carve watermelon into basket with handle. Scoop out 4 cups watermelon balls. Remove remaining watermelon pulp; drain basket shell. Combine watermelon balls with cantaloupe, honeydew, pineapple and strawberries in bowl. Combine yogurt, lemon juice and poppy seed in small serving bowl. Chill watermelon basket, fruit and dressing until serving time. Spoon fruit into basket. Serve with poppy seed dressing. Yield: 16 servings.

Approx Per Serving: Cal 52; Prot 1 g; Carbo 11 g; Fiber 1 g;
    T Fat <1 g; Chol 1 mg; Sod 15 mg.

Dietary Exchanges: Fruit 1

ORANGE AND PEAR MOLD

1 29-ounce can pears
2 3-ounce packages orange
   gelatin
1 3/4 cups boiling water
2 tablespoons lemon juice

2 tablespoons vinegar
2 tablespoons prepared
   horseradish
Salt to taste
1 cup finely chopped celery

Drain and chop pears, reserving juice. Dissolve gelatin in boiling water in medium bowl. Add lemon juice, vinegar, horseradish and salt; mix well. Add enough water to reserved pear juice to measure 1 1/4 cups. Stir into gelatin mixture. Chill until partially set. Fold in pears and celery. Pour into lightly oiled 1 1/2-quart mold. Chill until firm. Unmold onto serving plate. Yield: 8 servings.

Approx Per Serving: Cal 159; Prot 2 g; Carbo 40 g; Fiber 1 g;
    T Fat <1 g; Chol 0 mg; Sod 128 mg.

Dietary Exchanges: Fruit 1 1/2; Bread/Starch 1

☎ Substitute mayonnaise-type salad dressing for mayonnaise when possible to cut calories and fat in half and reduce cholesterol.

PEACHES AND CREAM SALAD

1   3-ounce package lemon
    gelatin
1   3-ounce package orange
    gelatin

2 cups boiling water
2 cups vanilla ice cream,
  softened
4 peaches, peeled, sliced

Dissolve lemon gelatin and orange gelatin in boiling water in bowl. Add ice cream; stir until melted. Chill until partially set. Fold in peaches. Spoon into mold. Chill until set. Unmold onto serving plate. Yield: 12 servings.

Approx Per Serving: Cal 110; Prot 2 g; Carbo 21 g; Fiber 1 g;
    T Fat 2 g; Chol 10 mg; Sod 64 mg.

Dietary Exchanges: Fruit 1/2; Bread/Starch 1; Fat 1/2

PINEAPPLE AND COTTAGE CHEESE MOLD

2 teaspoons unflavored
  gelatin
3 tablespoons cold water
1 cup pineapple juice
2 tablespoons lemon juice

2 tablespoons sugar
1/2 cup crushed pineapple
1/3 cup finely chopped celery
1/3 cup cottage cheese

Soften gelatin in cold water in medium bowl. Heat mixture of pineapple juice and lemon juice just to the boiling point in saucepan. Add to gelatin; stir until gelatin is dissolved. Stir in sugar. Chill until partially set. Fold in pineapple, celery and cottage cheese. Spoon into mold. Chill until firm. Unmold onto serving plate. Yield: 8 servings.

Approx Per Serving: Cal 60; Prot 4 g; Carbo 10 g; Fiber <1 g;
    T Fat <1 g; Chol 1 mg; Sod 44 mg.

Dietary Exchanges: Fruit 1

STRAWBERRY FRUIT MOLD

1 6-ounce package
   strawberry gelatin
2 cups boiling water
2 bananas, sliced
1 8-ounce can crushed
   pineapple

2 10-ounce packages frozen
   strawberries
1/2 cup chopped walnuts
1 cup sour cream substitute

Dissolve gelatin in boiling water in bowl. Add bananas, undrained pineapple, strawberries and walnuts; mix gently. Spoon half the mixture into glass dish. Chill until firm. Spread sour cream substitute over congealed layer. Spoon remaining gelatin over top. Chill until firm. Cut into squares. May use one 3-ounce package strawberry gelatin and one 3-ounce package lime gelatin for a holiday salad. Yield: 12 servings.

Approx Per Serving: Cal 177; Prot 3 g; Carbo 31 g; Fiber 2 g;
   T Fat 6 g; Chol 0 mg; Sod 66 mg.

Dietary Exchanges: Fruit 1 1/2; Bread/Starch 1; Fat 1 1/2

SUMMER FRUIT SALAD

1 cup cantaloupe balls
1 cup blueberries
1 cup green grape halves
1 cup strawberries

3/4 cup orange juice
1/4 cup white grape juice
2 tablespoons lemon juice
1/4 cup white wine

Combine cantaloupe, blueberries, grapes and strawberries in bowl; mix gently. Combine orange juice, grape juice, lemon juice and wine in small bowl; mix well. Pour over fruit; mix gently. Chill until serving time. Yield: 4 servings.

Approx Per Serving: Cal 102; Prot 1 g; Carbo 23 g; Fiber 3 g;
   T Fat <1 g; Chol 0 mg; Sod 17 mg.

Dietary Exchanges: Fruit 1 1/2

TANGERINE SALAD

Sections of 4 tangerines
Sections of 1 grapefruit
1 unpeeled apple, chopped
2 tablespoons tangerine juice

2 tablespoons sugar
1 cup plain low-fat yogurt
1 banana, sliced
1/4 cup sliced toasted almonds

Combine tangerines, grapefruit and apple in bowl; mix well. Blend tangerine juice, sugar and yogurt in bowl; mix well. Fold into fruit. Chill for 1 hour or longer. Fold in banana. Serve on lettuce-lined serving plate. Sprinkle with almonds. Yield: 6 servings.

Approx Per Serving: Cal 142; Prot 4 g; Carbo 26 g; Fiber 3 g;
   T Fat 4 g; Chol 2 mg; Sod 28 mg.

Dietary Exchanges: Milk 1/2; Fruit 1 1/2; Meat 1/2; Fat 1/2

WINTER FRUIT SALAD

1 16-ounce can pineapple
   chunks, drained
4 red Delicious apples,
   chopped

4 cups green seedless grapes
Sections of 2 Navel oranges
1 banana, sliced
2 cups plain low-fat yogurt

Combine pineapple, apples, grapes, oranges and banana in bowl; mix gently. Stir in yogurt gently. Chill until serving time. Yield: 10 servings.

Approx Per Serving: Cal 122; Prot 3 g; Carbo 27 g; Fiber 3 g;
   T Fat 1 g; Chol 3 mg; Sod 34 mg.

Dietary Exchanges: Milk 1/2; Fruit 1 1/2

☎ Combine 1 1/2 cups vegetable juice cocktail, 2 tablespoons vinegar, 1 teaspoon prepared mustard, 1 teaspoon Worcestershire sauce and paprika to taste in bottle or jar; shake until well mixed. Use **Zesty Tomato Dressing** over lettuce wedges, assorted greens or even fresh citrus sections.

HUNAN BROCCOLI AND BEEF SALAD

6 cups broccoli flowerets
2 tablespoons oil
1 cup red bell pepper strips
1 cup green bell pepper strips
2 cups sliced mushrooms
1 pound rare roast beef, cut into strips

1 8-ounce can sliced water chestnuts, drained
1/4 cup vinegar
1/4 cup reduced-sodium soy sauce
Dried hot peppers to taste

Stir-fry broccoli in hot oil in wok for 2 minutes. Cook, covered, for 2 minutes; remove to serving bowl. Stir-fry bell pepper strips for 2 minutes; add to broccoli. Stir-fry mushrooms for 3 minutes; add to broccoli. Add beef strips and water chestnuts to vegetables. Stir in vinegar, soy sauce and hot peppers. Chill until serving time. Yield: 8 servings.

Approx Per Serving: Cal 164; Prot 15 g; Carbo 12 g; Fiber 5 g; T Fat 7 g; Chol 30 mg; Sod 442 mg.

Dietary Exchanges: Vegetable 2 1/2; Meat 1 1/2; Fat 1/2

CURRIED CHICKEN SALAD

4 cups chopped cooked chicken
1 8-ounce can sliced water chestnuts, drained
1 cup chopped celery
2 cups pineapple chunks
1 apple, chopped

1 cup chopped walnuts
1 cup reduced-calorie mayonnaise
1 teaspoon soy sauce
1 tablespoon lemon juice
1/2 teaspoon pepper
1/2 teaspoon curry powder

Combine chicken, water chestnuts, celery, pineapple, apple and walnuts in bowl; mix well. Blend mayonnaise, soy sauce, lemon juice, pepper and curry powder in small bowl. Add to chicken mixture; mix lightly. Chill for 2 hours. Serve on lettuce-lined plates. Yield: 10 servings.

Approx Per Serving: Cal 206; Prot 16 g; Carbo 13 g; Fiber 2 g T Fat 11 g; Chol 42 mg; Sod 150 mg.

Dietary Exchanges: Vegetable 1/2; Fruit 1/2; Meat 2; Fat 2

GRILLED CHICKEN CAESAR SALAD

2 slices rye bread, crusts
  trimmed, cubed
1 tablespoon extra-virgin
  olive oil
1 pound chicken breast filets
Salt and pepper to taste
4 anchovy filets
2 tablespoons minced garlic

2 tablespoons lemon juice
1 tablespoon Dijon mustard
2 dashes of red pepper sauce
1/3 cup extra-virgin olive oil
1 head romaine lettuce, torn
3 tablespoons Parmesan
  cheese

Toast bread cubes in 1 tablespoon olive oil in skillet for 5 minutes, stirring constantly. Drain on paper towel. Rinse chicken and pat dry. Sprinkle with salt and pepper. Place on lightly oiled rack in broiler pan. Broil 3 inches from heat source in preheated broiler for 5 to 6 minutes or until tender, turning once. Cool for 5 minutes. Cut cross grain into 1/4-inch thick slices. Mash anchovy filets with garlic in large salad bowl. Add lemon juice, mustard, red pepper sauce, salt and pepper; mix well. Whisk in remaining 1/3 cup olive oil. Add chicken; toss to coat well. Add lettuce, cheese and bread cubes; toss to mix well. Yield: 4 servings.

Approx Per Serving: Cal 433; Prot 31 g; Carbo 9 g; Fiber 2 g;
  T Fat 30 g; Chol 76 mg; Sod 435 mg.

Dietary Exchanges: Vegetable 1/2; Bread/Starch 1/2; Meat 3 1/2; Fat 4 1/2

CHICKEN AND RICE SALAD

2 cups instant rice
1 cup chopped cooked
  chicken
1   16-ounce can kidney
  beans, drained
Whites of 3 hard-boiled eggs,
  chopped

1 small onion, chopped
3 tablespoons sweet pickle
  relish
Salt to taste
3 tablespoons reduced-
  calorie mayonnaise-type
  salad dressing

Cook rice using package directions. Cool to room temperature. Combine with chicken, beans, egg whites, onion, relish and salt in bowl; mix well. Add salad dressing; toss lightly to mix.
Yield: 6 servings.

Approx Per Serving: Cal 369; Prot 17 g; Carbo 68 g; Fiber 5 g;
  T Fat 3 g; Chol 17 mg; Sod 375 mg.

Dietary Exchanges: Vegetable 1/2; Bread/Starch 4; Meat 1; Fat 1/2

SKINNY CHICKEN SALAD

2 cups chopped cooked
    chicken
1 cup diagonally sliced celery
1 clove of garlic, minced

1 tablespoon soy sauce
1 tablespoon sesame seed oil
1 teaspoon vinegar
Salt to taste

Combine chicken, celery and garlic in bowl. Add soy sauce, oil, vinegar and salt; toss lightly. Yield: 2 servings.

Approx Per Serving: Cal 300; Prot 35 g; Carbo 4 g; Fiber <1 g;
    T Fat 16 g; Chol 96 mg; Sod 648 mg.

Dietary Exchanges: Vegetable 1/2; Meat 4 1/2; Fat 1 1/2

SOUTHWESTERN CHICKEN SALAD

1 tablespoon fresh lime juice
1 teaspoon olive oil
1/4 teaspoon minced garlic
1 teaspoon chopped fresh
    thyme
Salt and freshly ground
    pepper to taste
1 pound chicken breast filets
3 tablespoons fresh lime juice
2 teaspoons honey
2 teaspoons olive oil
1/2 clove of garlic, crushed

6 cups torn lettuce
1 small red bell pepper,
    sliced into rings
1/2 cantaloupe, thinly sliced
2/3 cup fresh or frozen corn
1 small tomato, chopped
1 green onion, thinly sliced
2 tablespoons chopped fresh
    cilantro
2 teaspoons minced jalapeño
    pepper

Combine first 5 ingredients in 10-inch glass dish. Rinse chicken and pat dry. Add to marinade, turning to coat well. Let stand for 15 minutes. Microwave, loosely covered, on High for 4 to 4 1/2 minutes or until cooked through, turning once. Let stand for several minutes. Whisk 3 tablespoons lime juice, honey, 2 teaspoons olive oil, 1/2 clove of garlic, salt and pepper in small bowl. Slice chicken into 1/2-inch wide strips. Combine with 2 tablespoons honey mixture in bowl; mix well. Add lettuce, red pepper and cantaloupe; toss to coat well. Spoon onto serving platter. Mix remaining honey mixture with corn, tomato, green onion, cilantro and jalapeño pepper. Spoon over chicken mixture. Garnish with cilantro sprigs and lime wedges. Yield: 4 servings.

Approx Per Serving: Cal 275; Prot 30 g; Carbo 23 g; Fiber 4 g
    T Fat 7 g; Chol 72 mg; Sod 191 mg.

Dietary Exchanges: Vegetable 1 1/2; Fruit 1/2; Bread/Starch 1/2; Meat 3; Fat 1

FRUITED TURKEY AND SEAFOOD SALAD

2 cups chopped cooked
   turkey
1 cup seedless green grape
   halves
1 cup chopped cantaloupe
1 8-ounce can sliced water
   chestnuts, drained
4 ounces cooked crab meat

8 ounces cooked peeled
   shrimp
1 small banana
1/3 cup reduced-calorie
   mayonnaise-type salad
   dressing
1 tablespoon lemon juice

Combine turkey, grapes, cantaloupe, water chestnuts, crab meat and shrimp in large salad bowl; mix well. Chill, covered, for several hours. Mash banana in small bowl. Stir in salad dressing and lemon juice. Chill, covered, until serving time. Spoon salad onto lettuce-lined serving plates. Drizzle with dressing. Yield: 6 servings.

Approx Per Serving: Cal 184; Prot 22 g; Carbo 16 g; Fiber 1 g;
   T Fat 4 g; Chol 97 mg; Sod 213 mg.

Dietary Exchanges: Vegetable 1; Fruit 1/2; Meat 2 1/2; Fat 1/2

ZESTY BROCCOLI AND HAM SALAD

1 1/2 pounds fresh broccoli,
   trimmed, coarsely chopped
1 1/2 cups chopped cooked
   ham
1/2 cup shredded Swiss
   cheese
1/4 cup chopped red bell
   pepper

1/4 cup chopped green onions
1/2 cup reduced-calorie Italian
   salad dressing
1/4 cup cider vinegar
1 tablespoon Dijon mustard
1/2 teaspoon savory
Freshly ground pepper to
   taste

Combine broccoli, ham, cheese, red pepper and green onions in large serving bowl; toss to mix well. Combine salad dressing, vinegar, mustard, savory and pepper in small bowl; mix well. Add to salad; toss gently. Chill, covered, for 8 hours to overnight. Yield: 6 servings.

Approx Per Serving: Cal 154; Prot 14 g; Carbo 8 g; Fiber 4 g;
   T Fat 8 g; Chol 31 mg; Sod 771 mg.

Dietary Exchanges: Vegetable 1 1/2; Meat 1 1/2; Fat 1

SUMMER LAMB SALAD

¼ cup oil
¼ cup vinegar
1 tablespoon sugar
1 tablespoon minced onion
1 teaspoon oregano
Salt and pepper to taste

3 cups chopped cooked lamb
2 cups torn lettuce
2 cups torn endive
2 cups torn spinach
2 tomatoes, cut into wedges

Combine oil, vinegar, sugar, onion, oregano, salt and pepper in salad bowl; mix well. Add lamb; toss to coat well. Chill for 1 hour or longer. Add lettuce, endive, spinach and tomatoes; toss gently. Garnish with hard-boiled egg slices. Yield: 8 servings.

Approx Per Serving: Cal 173; Prot 13 g; Carbo 5 g; Fiber 2 g;
   T Fat 12 g; Chol 42 mg; Sod 50 mg.

Dietary Exchanges: Vegetable ½; Meat 1½; Fat 1½

CRAB MEAT SALAD

8 ounces cooked crab meat
1 tablespoon chopped green
   onions
1 tablespoon chopped fresh
   parsley
2 tablespoons plain low-fat
   yogurt

1 tablespoon reduced-calorie
   mayonnaise
1 teaspoon lemon juice
Pepper to taste
2 Bibb lettuce leaves
4 cherry tomatoes, cut into
   halves

Combine crab meat, green onions and parsley in bowl; mix well. Combine yogurt, mayonnaise, lemon juice and pepper in small bowl; mix well. Add to crab mixture; toss gently. Chill, covered, until serving time. Spoon into lettuce cups. Arrange cherry tomato halves around salad. Yield: 2 servings.

Approx Per Serving: Cal 172; Prot 23 g; Carbo 8 g; Fiber 3 g;
   T Fat 5 g; Chol 116 mg; Sod 596 mg.

Dietary Exchanges: Vegetable 1½; Meat 2½; Fat ½

1885

CRAB AND GRAPEFRUIT SALAD

1 7-ounce can crab meat
1 cup chopped celery
1/4 cup lemon juice
Salt and onion powder to
    taste

Sections of 2 grapefruit
2 tomatoes, sliced into
    wedges

Combine crab meat, celery, lemon juice, salt and onion powder in bowl; mix well. Spoon into center of lettuce-lined serving plate. Arrange grapefruit sections and tomatoes around outer edge. Yield: 4 servings.

Approx Per Serving: Cal 109; Prot 10 g; Carbo 15 g; Fiber 3 g;
    T Fat 1 g; Chol 50 mg; Sod 280 mg.

Dietary Exchanges: Vegetable 1; Fruit 1; Meat 1

TOMATOES STUFFED WITH CRAB SALAD

4 tomatoes
1 7-ounce can crab meat
1/2 cup chopped celery
1 tablespoon lemon juice
2 tablespoons capers

1/4 cup reduced-calorie
    mayonnaise-type salad
    dressing
Salt and pepper to taste

Scoop pulp from tomatoes, reserving shells. Chop pulp. Combine with crab meat, celery, lemon juice, capers, salad dressing, salt and pepper in bowl; mix well. Spoon into tomato shells. Yield: 4 servings.

Approx Per Serving: Cal 97; Prot 10 g; Carbo 9 g; Fiber 2 g;
    T Fat 3 g; Chol 52 mg; Sod 315 mg.

Dietary Exchanges: Vegetable 1; Meat 1; Fat 1

☎ Water-pack tuna has 300 fewer calories per 61/2-ounce can than tuna packed in oil. It is also lower in fat and cholesterol.

SHRIMP SALAD

1 16-ounce can cut green
   beans
2 chicken bouillon cubes
2/3 cup uncooked rice
1 clove of garlic
1 tablespoon oil
1/4 teaspoon dry mustard

1/2 teaspoon sugar
1/4 cup vinegar
1 7-ounce can shrimp,
   drained
2/3 cup sliced celery
1/2 cup chopped onion
2 cups torn lettuce

Drain beans, reserving liquid. Add enough water to reserved bean liquid to measure 2 cups. Bring to a boil in saucepan. Stir in bouillon until dissolved. Add rice. Bring to a boil; reduce heat. Simmer, covered, for 15 minutes or until tender. Chill in refrigerator. Crush garlic in large salad bowl. Add oil, dry mustard, sugar, vinegar, shrimp and beans; toss to mix well. Chill until serving time. Add rice to shrimp mixture; mix well. Add celery, onion and lettuce; toss lightly. Yield: 4 servings.

Approx Per Serving: Cal 246; Prot 16 g; Carbo 35 g; Fiber 3 g;
    T Fat 5 g; Chol 86 mg; Sod 968 mg.

Dietary Exchanges: Vegetable 1 1/2; Bread/Starch 1 1/2; Meat 1 1/2; Fat 1/2

TUNA SALAD

1 6-ounce can water-pack
   tuna
2 small stalks celery, chopped
1/2 carrot, shredded
1/2 small onion, finely chopped
1 tablespoon chopped pickle

1/2 apple, chopped
1/4 cup chopped pecans
1 tablespoon reduced-calorie
   mayonnaise
1 teaspoon mustard
1 teaspoon lemon juice

Combine tuna, celery, carrot, onion, pickle, apple and pecans in serving bowl. Add mayonnaise, mustard and lemon juice; mix well. Chill until serving time. May use tuna drained or undrained. Yield: 4 servings.

Approx Per Serving: Cal 138; Prot 12 g; Carbo 7 g; Fiber 2 g;
    T Fat 7 g; Chol 19 mg; Sod 204 mg.

Dietary Exchanges: Vegetable 1/2; Meat 1 1/2; Fat 1 1/2

TUNA VEGETABLE SLAW

1   7-ounce can water-pack
    tuna, drained
1 cup shredded cabbage
1 cup cooked peas
1/2 cup chopped celery
1/4 cup shredded carrot

1/2 cup chopped green bell
    pepper
1 tablespoon minced onion
1/4 cup mayonnaise
1 tablespoon lemon juice
Salt to taste

Combine tuna with cabbage, peas, celery, carrot, green pepper and onion in bowl; mix well. Blend mayonnaise, lemon juice and salt in small bowl. Add to salad; toss lightly. Yield: 6 servings.

Approx Per Serving: Cal 141; Prot 11 g; Carbo 6 g; Fiber 2 g;
    T Fat 8 g; Chol 19 mg; Sod 257 mg.

Dietary Exchanges: Vegetable 1/2; Bread/Starch 1/2; Meat 1; Fat 1 1/2

FRUITED PASTA SALAD

8 ounces uncooked
    acini-de-pepe pasta
1/2 cup sugar
2 teaspoons flour
1 3/4 cups pineapple juice
2 eggs, beaten
Salt to taste
1 tablespoon lemon juice

3   8-ounce cans mandarin
    oranges, drained
2   20-ounce cans pineapple
    chunks, drained
1   16-ounce can crushed
    pineapple, drained
1 cup coconut
8 ounces whipped topping

Cook pasta using package directions; drain. Combine sugar, flour, pineapple juice, eggs and salt in saucepan. Cook until thickened, stirring constantly. Combine with lemon juice and pasta in airtight container; mix well. Chill overnight. Fold in oranges, pineapple chunks, crushed pineapple, coconut and whipped topping at serving time. Yield: 24 servings.

Approx Per Serving: Cal 150; Prot 2 g; Carbo 27 g; Fiber 2 g;
    T Fat 4 g; Chol 23 mg; Sod 12 mg.

Dietary Exchanges: Fruit 1; Bread/Starch 1; Fat 1

GARBANZO PASTA SALAD

4 ounces uncooked spinach
   pasta
1 15-ounce can garbanzo
   beans
1/2 cup chopped celery
1/3 cup chopped red bell
   pepper
2 tablespoons chopped
   chives

1/3 cup shredded carrot
3 tablespoons white wine
   vinegar
2 tablespoons reduced-
   calorie mayonnaise
1 tablespoon olive oil
2 tablespoons Dijon mustard
1/4 teaspoon salt
1/4 teaspoon pepper

Cook pasta using package directions, omitting salt; drain and cool. Rinse garbanzo beans in cold water in colander for 1 minute. Drain for 1 minute. Combine pasta, beans, celery, bell pepper, chives and carrot in large bowl; toss lightly to mix well. Combine vinegar, mayonnaise, olive oil, mustard, salt and pepper in small bowl. Blend with whisk. Add to salad; toss lightly. Chill, covered, in refrigerator. Serve on lettuce-lined plates. Garnish with tomato wedges. Yield: 4 servings.

Approx Per Serving: Cal 279; Prot 10 g; Carbo 41 g; Fiber 8 g;
   T Fat 9 g; Chol 3 mg; Sod 674 mg.

Dietary Exchanges: Vegetable 1/2; Bread/Starch 2 1/2; Meat 1/2; Fat 1 1/2

CONFETTI PASTA SALAD

1 12-ounce package spiral
   pasta, cooked
1 cucumber, chopped
2 tomatoes, chopped
8 green onions, sliced

1/2 bottle of salad supreme
   seasoning
1 12-ounce bottle of Italian
   salad dressing

Combine pasta, cucumber, tomatoes and green onions in salad bowl; mix well. Mix salad supreme seasoning and salad dressing in small bowl. Add to salad; mix gently. Yield: 15 servings.

Approx Per Serving: Cal 198; Prot 3 g; Carbo 21 g; Fiber 2 g;
   T Fat 11 g; Chol 0 mg; Sod 181 mg.
   Nutritional information does not include salad supreme seasoning.

Dietary Exchanges: Vegetable 1/2; Bread/Starch 1 1/2; Fat 2 1/2

CRUNCHY RICE SALAD

1/3 cup reduced-calorie
  mayonnaise
1/3 cup plain low-fat yogurt
1/4 cup honey
2 tablespoons Dijon mustard
Salt to taste
3 cups cooked rice

1 1/2 cups coarsely chopped
  fresh snow peas
1 cup thinly sliced celery
1 8-ounce can sliced water
  chestnuts, drained
1/2 cup slivered almonds
Paprika to taste

Blend mayonnaise, yogurt, honey, mustard and salt in large bowl; mix well. Add rice, snow peas, celery, water chestnuts and almonds; mix lightly. Chill, covered, for several hours. Sprinkle with paprika. Yield: 6 servings.

Approx Per Serving: Cal 277; Prot 6 g; Carbo 44 g; Fiber 4 g;
  T Fat 9 g; Chol 5 mg; Sod 103 mg.

Dietary Exchanges: Vegetable 1; Bread/Starch 1 1/2; Meat 1/2; Fat 2

RICE AND PEA SALAD

2 16-ounce cans peas
1 1/2 cups rice, cooked
1 1/2 cups chopped celery
1 cup sliced mushrooms
2 tablespoons lemon juice

3/4 cup mayonnaise-type
  salad dressing
1/3 cup minced onion
Salt and pepper to taste

Drain peas, reserving 1/4 cup liquid. Combine peas with rice, celery and mushrooms in bowl; mix well. Blend reserved pea liquid, lemon juice, mayonnaise, onion, salt and pepper in bowl. Add to salad; mix well. Chill until serving time. Yield: 15 servings.

Approx Per Serving: Cal 160; Prot 4 g; Carbo 26 g; Fiber 3 g;
  T Fat 4 g; Chol 3 mg; Sod 227 mg.

Dietary Exchanges: Bread/Starch 1 1/2; Fat 1 1/2

SPAGHETTI SALAD

1 12-ounce package
  spaghetti
1 purple onion, chopped
2 tomatoes, chopped
2 cucumbers, sliced

1 green bell pepper, chopped
1 tablespoon salad supreme
  seasoning
1 8-ounce bottle of oil-free
  Italian salad dressing

Cook spaghetti using package directions; drain. Combine with onion, tomatoes, cucumbers, green pepper and salad supreme seasoning in bowl; mix well. Add salad dressing; toss to mix well. Chill until serving time. Yield: 10 servings.

Approx Per Serving: Cal 171; Prot 5 g; Carbo 31 g; Fiber 3 g;
    T Fat 3 g; Chol 2 mg; Sod 183 mg.

Dietary Exchanges: Vegetable 1; Bread/Starch 2; Fat 1

TABOULI

3/4 cup bulgur
2 cups water
3 large tomatoes, chopped
3 tablespoons minced parsley
2 tablespoons sliced green
  onions

1 teaspoon salt
2 tablespoons oil
2 tablespoons lemon juice
3 cups finely shredded lettuce
Salt and pepper to taste

Soak bulgur in water in bowl for 30 minutes. Drain well, squeezing out excess liquid. Add tomatoes, parsley, green onions and 1 teaspoon salt. Add mixture of oil and lemon juice; mix well. Chill until serving time. Add lettuce, salt and pepper just before serving. May increase amount of parsley and omit lettuce if preferred. Yield: 6 servings.

Approx Per Serving: Cal 137; Prot 3 g; Carbo 21 g; Fiber 2 g;
    T Fat 5 g; Chol 0 mg; Sod 334 mg.

Dietary Exchanges: Vegetable 1; Bread/Starch 1; Fat 1

CHILLED ASPARAGUS SALAD

1 cucumber, chopped
1 Vidalia onion, chopped
1 tomato, cut into quarters
1 16-ounce can asparagus,
  chilled, drained

4 slices crisp-fried bacon
1 teaspoon chopped dill
1/4 cup ranch salad dressing

Combine cucumber, onion and tomato in shallow dish. Top with asparagus and bacon. Sprinkle with dill. Drizzle with salad dressing. Yield: 4 servings.

Approx Per Serving: Cal 143; Prot 6 g; Carbo 10 g; Fiber 4 g;
  T Fat 10 g; Chol 5 mg; Sod 627 mg.

Dietary Exchanges: Vegetable 2; Meat 1/2; Fat 2

BLACK-EYED PEA SALAD

3 16-ounce cans black-eyed
  peas, drained
1 2-ounce jar chopped
  pimento, drained
1/2 cup chopped purple onion
1/4 cup white vinegar

6 tablespoons red wine
  vinegar
6 tablespoons sugar
6 tablespoons oil
3/4 teaspoon red pepper
1/4 teaspoon salt

Combine black-eyed peas, pimento and onion in salad bowl; mix gently. Combine white vinegar, wine vinegar, sugar, oil, red pepper and salt in small bowl; mix well. Pour over salad; mix gently. Chill, covered, for 3 hours. Yield: 8 servings.

Approx Per Serving: Cal 314; Prot 14 g; Carbo 42 g; Fiber 12 g;
  T Fat 12 g; Chol 0 mg; Sod 69 mg.

Dietary Exchanges: Bread/Starch 2 1/2; Fat 2

☎ Omit bacon and use reduced-calorie salad dressing to reduce fat, cholesterol, sodium and calories in **Chilled Asparagus Salad.**

BROCCOLI SALAD

1 bunch broccoli
8 ounces cauliflower, chopped
1 cup sliced black olives
4 ounces Cheddar cheese,
   cubed
1/4 cup chopped onion
1 tomato, peeled, chopped
1 cup reduced-calorie Italian
   salad dressing

Blanch broccoli in boiling water for 1 minute; drain. Separate flowerets; chop stems. Combine with cauliflower, olives, cheese, onion and tomato in salad bowl. Add salad dressing; mix well. Chill for 12 to 24 hours. May add 1 cup cooked pasta. Yield: 8 servings.

Approx Per Serving: Cal 148; Prot 6 g; Carbo 7 g; Fiber 3 g;
   T Fat 13 g; Chol 17 mg; Sod 478 mg.

Dietary Exchanges: Vegetable 1; Meat 1/2; Fat 3

TART AND CREAMY COLESLAW

1 small head cabbage,
   shredded
2 tablespoons chopped onion
1/4 cup chopped green bell
   pepper
1/2 cup shredded carrot
1/2 teaspoon sugar substitute
1 teaspoon lemon juice
1/3 cup plain low-fat yogurt

Combine vegetables in salad bowl. Add sugar substitute, lemon juice and yogurt; mix well. Chill until serving time. Yield: 6 servings.

Approx Per Serving: Cal 28; Prot 2 g; Carbo 5 g; Fiber 2 g;
   T Fat <1 g; Chol <1 mg; Sod 23 mg.

Dietary Exchanges: Vegetable 1

CORN SALAD

2 16-ounce cans Shoe Peg
   corn, drained
2 tomatoes, chopped
2 green onions, chopped
1 hot green pepper, chopped
2 tablespoons mayonnaise

Combine first 4 ingredients in bowl; mix well. Add mayonnaise; mix well. Chill until serving time. Yield: 6 servings.

Approx Per Serving: Cal 165; Prot 5 g; Carbo 31 g; Fiber 3 g
   T Fat 5 g; Chol 3 mg; Sod 461 mg.

Dietary Exchanges: Vegetable 1/2; Bread/Starch 2; Fat 1

FIRE AND ICE

6 large tomatoes, peeled, cut
   into quarters
1 green bell pepper, sliced
   into strips
1 medium onion, sliced into
   rings
3/4 cup white vinegar

1/4 cup water
1 tablespoon sugar
1 1/2 teaspoons cayenne
   pepper
1 1/2 teaspoons mustard seed
Salt and pepper to taste
1 cucumber, sliced

Combine tomatoes, green pepper and onion in bowl. Combine vinegar, water, sugar, cayenne pepper, mustard seed, salt and pepper in saucepan. Bring to a boil. Cook for 1 minute. Pour over vegetables in bowl. Chill in refrigerator. Add cucumber at serving time. Yield: 6 servings.

Approx Per Serving: Cal 50; Prot 2 g; Carbo 13 g; Fiber 3 g;
   T Fat <1 g; Chol 0 mg; Sod 12 mg.

Dietary Exchanges: Vegetable 1 1/2

MOLDED GAZPACHO SALAD

2 cups vegetable juice
   cocktail
2 3-ounce packages lemon
   gelatin
1 cup vegetable juice cocktail
1/4 cup vinegar
2 teaspoons Worcestershire
   sauce

1/4 teaspoon pepper
1 cup chopped celery
1/2 cup chopped green bell
   pepper
1/2 cup chopped cucumber
2 tablespoons minced onion
1/2 cup chopped parsley

Bring 2 cups vegetable juice cocktail to a boil in saucepan. Stir in gelatin until dissolved. Add 1 cup vegetable juice cocktail, vinegar, Worcestershire sauce and pepper; mix well. Chill until partially set. Stir in celery, green pepper, cucumber, onion and parsley. Spoon into oiled ring mold. Chill until set. Unmold onto serving plate. Yield: 10 servings.

Approx Per Serving: Cal 82; Prot 2 g; Carbo 20 g; Fiber 1 g;
   T Fat <1 g; Chol 0 mg; Sod 341 mg.

Dietary Exchanges: Vegetable 1; Bread/Starch 1

MAYAN SALAD

8 cups torn mixed iceberg
lettuce, romaine lettuce
and spinach
1 1/2 cups sliced water
chestnuts
1 medium red onion, thinly
sliced into rings
1 16-ounce can grapefruit
sections, drained
1 16-ounce can mandarin
oranges, drained

8 ounces cherry tomatoes,
cut into halves
3 tablespoons cider vinegar
2 tablespoons lime juice
6 tablespoons olive oil
1 clove of garlic
1/2 teaspoon cumin
1/8 teaspoon red pepper
1 teaspoon cracked pepper
1/2 teaspoon salt
1 large avocado

Combine salad greens and water chestnuts in salad bowl. Arrange onion rings, grapefruit sections, orange sections and tomato halves on greens. Chill, covered, for 1 to 2 hours. Combine vinegar, lime juice, olive oil, garlic and seasonings in blender container; process until smooth. Chill until serving time. Slice avocado over salad at serving time. Drizzle dressing over top; toss gently. Yield: 8 servings.

Approx Per Serving: Cal 220; Prot 3 g; Carbo 24 g; Fiber 4 g;
T Fat 14 g; Chol 0 mg; Sod 155 mg.

Dietary Exchanges: Vegetable 1 1/2; Fruit 1; Fat 3

HERBED POTATO SALAD

1/2 cup plain low-fat yogurt
1/4 cup reduced-calorie
mayonnaise
2 tablespoons chopped
parsley
1 tablespoon chopped green
onions

1 tablespoon chopped fresh
basil
3 medium potatoes, cooked,
chopped
1/2 cup frozen green peas,
thawed

Combine yogurt, mayonnaise, parsley, green onions and basil in bowl; mix well. Add potatoes and peas; mix lightly. Chill, covered, for several hours. Yield: 4 servings.

Approx Per Serving: Cal 194; Prot 5 g; Carbo 34 g; Fiber 4 g;
T Fat 5 g; Chol 7 mg; Sod 44 mg.

Dietary Exchanges: Milk 1/2; Bread/Starch 2; Fat 1

WILTED SPINACH SALAD

1 small red onion, cut into
 1/4-inch wedges
2 teaspoons olive oil
2 10-ounce packages
 stemmed fresh spinach

2 teaspoons balsamic vinegar
Salt and freshly ground
 pepper to taste

Combine onion and olive oil in 2 or 3-quart glass dish. Microwave, covered, on High for 2 minutes. Add spinach, pressing down well. Microwave, covered, for 2 minutes or until spinach begins to wilt. Stir to coat well. Microwave, covered for 2 to 3 minutes longer, or until tender. Sprinkle with vinegar, salt and pepper. Yield: 4 servings.

Approx Per Serving: Cal 60; Prot 4 g; Carbo 7 g; Fiber 5 g;
 T Fat 3 g; Chol 0 mg; Sod 112 mg.

Dietary Exchanges: Vegetable 2; Fat 1/2

TOMATO ASPIC

2 envelopes unflavored
 gelatin
3 1/4 cups tomato juice
1/4 teaspoon Tabasco sauce

1 teaspoon Worcestershire
 sauce
1/4 cup lemon juice
Salt to taste

Sprinkle gelatin over 1 cup tomato juice in saucepan. Cook over moderate heat until gelatin dissolves, stirring constantly; remove from heat. Stir in remaining 2 1/4 cups tomato juice. Add Tabasco sauce, Worcestershire sauce, lemon juice and salt; mix well. Pour into oiled 1-quart mold. Chill for 3 hours or until firm. Unmold onto serving plate. Fill center with cottage cheese or coleslaw. Yield: 6 servings.

Approx Per Serving: Cal 34; Prot 3 g; Carbo 7 g; Fiber 2 g;
 T Fat <1 g; Chol 0 mg; Sod 490 mg.

Dietary Exchanges: Vegetable 1

1880

CHINESE VEGETABLE SALAD

1   16-ounce can Chinese
    vegetables
1   16-ounce can seasoned
    green beans
1   8-ounce can sliced water
    chestnuts
1   16-ounce can green peas

1   8-ounce can sliced
    mushrooms
1½ cups chopped celery
1   onion, sliced into rings
½ cup sugar
¾ cup wine tarragon vinegar

Drain Chinese vegetables, green beans, water chestnuts, peas and mushrooms. Combine with celery and onion in bowl; mix well. Blend sugar and vinegar in small bowl. Pour over vegetables; toss to mix well. Chill overnight, stirring occasionally. Yield: 12 servings.

Approx Per Serving: Cal 107; Prot 4 g; Carbo 25 g; Fiber 4 g;
    T Fat <1 g; Chol 0 mg; Sod 206 mg.

Dietary Exchanges: Vegetable 2; Bread/Starch ½

WINTER SALAD WITH GRAPES AND ALMONDS

¼ cup raspberry vinegar
½ cup (or less) olive oil
2 cloves of garlic, crushed
½ teaspoon honey
Salt to taste
6 ounces spinach or romaine
    lettuce

½ cup julienne red bell
    pepper
½ cup julienne carrot
½ cup seedless grape halves
2 tablespoons slivered
    almonds, slightly toasted

Combine vinegar, olive oil, garlic, honey and salt in covered jar; shake to mix well. Combine spinach, red pepper, carrot, grapes and almonds in salad bowl. Add dressing; toss to mix well. Make raspberry vinegar by pressing 1 pint of fresh or frozen raspberries through a sieve and adding the juice to 2 cups of wine vinegar. Yield: 6 servings.

Approx Per Serving: Cal 191; Prot 1 g; Carbo 5 g; Fiber 1 g;
    T Fat 19 g; Chol 0 mg; Sod 6 mg.

Dietary Exchanges: Vegetable ½; Fat 4

HONEY MUSTARD DRESSING

1 cup plain low-fat yogurt   **1 tablespoon mustard**
1/2 teaspoon honey

     Combine all ingredients in bowl; mix well. Store in refrigerator. Use as salad dressing or vegetable dip. Yield: 16 tablespoons.

Approx Per Tablespoon: Cal 11; Prot 1 g; Carbo 1 g; Fiber <1 g;
    T Fat <1 g; Chol <1 mg; Sod 22 mg.

Dietary Exchanges: Free

ITALIAN DRESSING

3/4 cup lemon juice   **1/2 teaspoon seasoned salt**
1 1/2 tablespoons honey   **1 1/2 teaspoons parsley flakes**
3 cups water   **1 tablespoon onion flakes**
2 1/2 tablespoons cornstarch   **3/4 teaspoon celery seed**
1/2 teaspoon garlic powder   **1/2 teaspoon chili powder**
1 teaspoon basil

     Bring lemon juice, honey and 3 cups water to a boil in saucepan. Blend cornstarch with a small amount of water. Stir into boiling mixture. Cook until thickened, stirring constantly. Add remaining ingredients; mix well. Store in refrigerator. Yield: 64 tablespoons.

Approx Per Tablespoon: Cal 4; Prot <1 g; Carbo 1 g; Fiber <1 g;
    T Fat <1 g; Chol 0 mg; Sod 15 mg.

Dietary Exchanges: Free

GAZPACHO DRESSING

1 large tomato   **1/4 teaspoon sugar**
5 tablespoons peanut oil   **1/2 teaspoon oregano**
1 tablespoon olive oil   **1/2 teaspoon salt**
1 1/2 tablespoons vinegar   **Freshly ground pepper to**
1 clove of garlic, chopped   **taste**

     Peel and seed tomato; chop coarsely. Combine with oils, vinegar, garlic, sugar and seasonings in food processor container. Process until smooth. Store in refrigerator. Yield: 20 tablespoons.

Approx Per Tablespoon: Cal 37; Prot <1 g; Carbo <1 g; Fiber <1 g
    T Fat 4 g; Chol 0 mg; Sod 49 mg.

Dietary Exchanges: Fat 1

Meats
and Meatless Main Dishes

EYE-OF-ROUND ROAST WITH VEGETABLES

1   2-pound eye-of-round
    roast, trimmed
3 medium carrots, cut into
    2-inch pieces
8 ounces new potatoes,
    peeled, cut into eighths
1 medium onion, coarsely
    chopped
2 stalks celery, cut into
    4-inch pieces

1 tablespoon reduced-
    sodium soy sauce
1/2 cup dry red wine
1/2 cup beef stock
1/2 teaspoon freshly ground
    pepper
1 tablespoon cornstarch
1/4 cup cold water
1/2 cup chopped parsley

Place roast in oven-roasting bag. Add carrots, potatoes, onion, celery, soy sauce, wine, beef stock and pepper; secure bag. Place in baking pan; pierce several holes in top of bag. Roast at 325 degrees for 1 hour. Cool for 10 to 15 minutes. Remove roast to carving board. Pour drippings into saucepan; place vegetables in bowl. Skim drippings. Spoon a small amount of drippings over roast. Let stand for 10 minutes. Stir mixture of cornstarch and water into remaining drippings in saucepan. Cook until thickened, stirring constantly. Pour into gravy bowl. Slice roast cross grain; place on warm serving platter. Arrange vegetables around roast. Sprinkle with parsley. Serve with gravy. Yield: 8 servings.

Approx Per Serving: Cal 224; Prot 20 g; Carbo 12 g; Fiber 2 g;
    T Fat 9 g; Chol 54 mg; Sod 226 mg.

Dietary Exchanges: Vegetable 1; Bread/Starch 1/2; Meat 21/2; Fat 1/2

☎ Reduce calories, fat and cholesterol in stock by chilling it
    and discarding any fat that solidifies on the surface.

MICROWAVE ITALIAN POT ROAST

1 onion, chopped
3 carrots, chopped
1 stalk celery, chopped
1 cup cut green beans
2 cloves of garlic, finely
  chopped
1 tablespoon olive oil
2 tablespoons tomato paste

1 bay leaf
1/8 teaspoon thyme
1/2 cup beef stock
1/2 cup dry red wine
Salt and pepper to taste
1 3-pound rump roast
1 tablespoon tomato paste
2 cups cooked rice

Combine first 6 ingredients in 3-quart glass dish. Microwave, covered, on High for 3 to 4 minutes, stirring once. Stir in 2 tablespoons tomato paste, bay leaf, thyme, beef stock, wine, salt and pepper. Place roast fat side up in dish. Microwave, covered, on High for 15 minutes, turning dish once. Turn roast over and baste. Microwave, covered, on Medium for 1 hour or until tender, turning roast over, basting and rotating dish once. Place roast on serving platter. Let stand, covered, for 10 minutes. Stir 1 tablespoon tomato paste into pan juices. Microwave on High for 5 minutes or until thickened, stirring twice. Slice beef thinly. Serve with sauce and rice. Yield: 8 servings.

Approx Per Serving: Cal 295; Prot 34 g; Carbo 18 g; Fiber 2 g;
    T Fat 8 g; Chol 81 mg; Sod 145 mg.

Dietary Exchanges: Vegetable 1 1/2; Bread/Starch 1/2; Meat 3 1/2; Fat 1/2

MARINATED BEEF TENDERLOIN

1 26-ounce bottle of very
  dry Sherry
2 cloves of garlic, chopped
1/4 cup Worcestershire sauce

1 cup reduced-sodium soy
  sauce
1 5-pound beef tenderloin
1/4 cup olive oil

Combine first 4 ingredients in large bowl. Add tenderloin. Marinate in refrigerator for 24 to 48 hours. Drain and pat dry. Coat with olive oil. Place on foil-lined wire rack, folding foil up around tenderloin. Preheat oven to 500 degrees. Reduce temperature to 350 degrees. Roast beef for 15 to 30 minutes or until done to taste. Yield: 12 servings.

Approx Per Serving: Cal 393; Prot 37 g; Carbo 7 g; Fiber 0 g
    T Fat 16 g; Chol 100 mg; Sod 1151 mg.
    Nutritional information includes entire amount of marinade.

Dietary Exchanges: Meat 4 1/2; Fat 1

BROILED FLANK STEAK

1 2-pound flank steak
2 tablespoons olive oil
1 clove of garlic, chopped
2 tablespoons reduced-
    sodium soy sauce

3 tablespoons red wine
1 1/2 teaspoons
    Worcestershire sauce
Oregano, rosemary and
    pepper to taste

Rub steak with olive oil. Combine garlic, soy sauce, wine, Worcestershire sauce and seasonings in shallow dish. Add flank steak, turning to coat well. Marinate at room temperature for 1 hour, turning occasionally. Place on rack in broiler pan. Broil 3 inches from heat source for 4 minutes on each side. Cut cross grain into thin slices. Yield: 6 servings.

Approx Per Serving: Cal 221; Prot 29 g; Carbo 1 g; Fiber 0 g;
    T Fat 10 g; Chol 72 mg; Sod 333 mg.
    Nutritional information includes entire amount of marinade.

Dietary Exchanges: Meat 3 1/2; Fat 1

SIMPLY ELEGANT STEAK AND RICE

1 1/2 pounds boneless round
    steak, thinly sliced
1 1/2 tablespoons oil
1 onion, sliced into rings
1 4-ounce can sliced
    mushrooms

1 10-ounce can cream of
    mushroom soup
1/4 cup dry Sherry
1 1/2 teaspoons garlic salt

Brown steak in oil in skillet. Add onion rings. Sauté until tender-crisp. Drain mushrooms, reserving liquid. Combine reserved liquid with soup, Sherry and garlic salt in bowl; mix well. Stir into skillet. Add mushrooms. Simmer, covered, for 1 hour or until steak is tender. Serve over rice. Yield: 6 servings.

Approx Per Serving: Cal 247; Prot 23 g; Carbo 8 g; Fiber 1 g;
    T Fat 11 g; Chol 55 mg; Sod 430 mg.

Dietary Exchanges: Vegetable 1/2; Bread/Starch 1; Meat 2 1/2; Fat 2 1/2

SKILLET STEAK WITH POTATOES

1½ pounds round steak
¼ cup flour
2 teaspoons salt
¼ teaspoon pepper
2 tablespoons oil
1   10-ounce can beef broth
1 cup water
4 medium potatoes, thinly sliced
2 medium onions, thinly sliced

Cut steak into serving pieces. Coat well with mixture of flour, salt and pepper. Brown on both sides in oil in skillet. Add beef broth and water. Simmer, covered, for 30 minutes. Turn steak. Top with potatoes and onions. Simmer, covered, for 30 minutes or until potatoes are tender. Yield: 6 servings.

Approx Per Serving: Cal 305; Prot 25 g; Carbo 30 g; Fiber 4 g;
    T Fat 9 g; Chol 54 mg; Sod 857 mg.

Dietary Exchanges: Vegetable ½; Bread/Starch 1½; Meat 2½; Fat 1

SPANISH STEAK

2 pounds round steak
1 tablespoon dry mustard
3 tablespoons shortening
2 tablespoons chopped green bell pepper
1 tablespoon chopped onion
2 tablespoons chopped celery
2 cups chopped tomatoes
2 tablespoons chopped parsley
1 tablespoon Worcestershire sauce
Salt to taste

Cut steak into serving pieces. Pound dry mustard into both sides of steak with meat mallet. Brown on both sides in shortening in skillet. Add green pepper, onion, celery, tomatoes, parsley, Worcestershire sauce and salt; mix well. Spoon into 3-quart baking dish. Bake, covered, at 350 degrees for 2 hours. Yield: 8 servings.

Approx Per Serving: Cal 180; Prot 22 g; Carbo 2 g; Fiber 1 g;
    T Fat 9 g; Chol 54 mg; Sod 67 mg.

Dietary Exchanges: Vegetable ½; Meat 2½; Fat 1

BEEF BARBECUE

1 pound beef cubes
1 tablespoon mustard
1 tablespoon vinegar
1/2 cup catsup
2 tablespoons sugar

1 1/2 tablespoons
  Worcestershire sauce
1 tablespoon margarine
Salt and pepper to taste

Combine beef with mustard, vinegar, catsup, sugar, Worcestershire sauce, margarine, salt and pepper in slow cooker. Cook on High for 1 hour. Cook on Low for 4 to 8 hours or until of desired consistency. Yield: 4 servings.

Approx Per Serving: Cal 246; Prot 18 g; Carbo 15 g; Fiber <1 g;
  T Fat 12 g; Chol 54 mg; Sod 498 mg.

Dietary Exchanges: Meat 2 1/2; Fat 1

BEEF AND BROCCOLI STIR-FRY

8 ounces boneless beef steak
1 tablespoon cornstarch
1 tablespoon soy sauce
1 teaspoon sugar
2 teaspoons minced
  gingerroot
1 clove of garlic, minced

1 tablespoon cornstarch
3 tablespoons soy sauce
1 cup water
3 tablespoons oil
Flowerets of 1 pound broccoli
1 onion, coarsely chopped
1 carrot, sliced

Cut beef cross grain into thin slices. Combine 1 tablespoon cornstarch, 1 tablespoon soy sauce, sugar, gingerroot and garlic in bowl. Add beef; mix to coat well. Let stand for 15 minutes. Combine 1 tablespoon cornstarch and 3 tablespoons soy sauce with water in bowl; set aside. Heat 1 tablespoon oil in wok. Add beef. Stir-fry for 1 minute; remove to bowl. Heat remaining 2 tablespoons oil in wok. Add broccoli, onion and carrot. Stir-fry for 4 minutes or until tender-crisp. Add beef and reserved cornstarch mixture. Cook until thickened, stirring constantly. Yield: 4 servings.

Approx Per Serving: Cal 237; Prot 16 g; Carbo 17 g; Fiber 5 g;
  T Fat 13 g; Chol 27 mg; Sod 1090 mg.

Dietary Exchanges: Vegetable 2; Bread/Starch 1/2; Meat 1 1/2; Fat 2

RED FLANNEL HASH

2 cups chopped cooked beef
1½ cups chopped cooked
  beets
4 cups chopped cooked
  potatoes

1 medium onion, finely
  chopped
Salt and pepper to taste

Combine beef, beets, potatoes, onion, salt and pepper in bowl; mix well. Spoon into greased skillet. Cook until brown crust forms on bottom, loosening around edge and shaking skillet to prevent overbrowning. Yield: 6 servings.

Approx Per Serving: Cal 208; Prot 14 g; Carbo 29 g; Fiber 3 g;
    T Fat 4 g; Chol 34 mg; Sod 193 mg.

Dietary Exchanges: Vegetable 1; Bread/Starch 1½; Meat 1½

STEAK CANTONESE

1½ pounds boneless round
  steak
2 tablespoons oil
2 large tomatoes, coarsely
  chopped
2 medium green bell peppers,
  cut into strips

¼ cup soy sauce
½ teaspoon each ginger,
  garlic salt and pepper
1 tablespoon cornstarch
¼ cup water
1 beef bouillon cube

Slice steak diagonally cross grain into thin strips. Brown in oil in large skillet over high heat. Reduce heat. Stir in tomatoes, green peppers, soy sauce and seasonings. Simmer, covered, for 10 minutes. Blend cornstarch and water in small bowl. Stir into steak. Add bouillon cube. Cook until thickened, stirring constantly. Simmer, covered, for 10 minutes. Serve over rice cooked in bouillon. Yield: 6 servings.

Approx Per Serving: Cal 196; Prot 23 g; Carbo 6 g; Fiber 1 g;
    T Fat 9 g; Chol 54 mg; Sod 1049 mg.

Dietary Exchanges: Vegetable ½; Meat 2½; Fat 1

GINGER AND ORANGE BEEF

3 pounds flank steak
1/4 cup grated fresh gingerroot
1 tablespoon corn oil
3 cups diagonally sliced
  carrots
3 cups chopped red bell
  peppers
3 cups chopped green bell
  peppers

2 cups sliced water chestnuts
8 ounces snow peas, trimmed
2 tablespoons grated orange
  rind
1 tablespoon cinnamon
1/2 cup reduced-sodium soy
  sauce
1 tablespoon cornstarch

Slice steak into 1/4-inch thick strips. Stir-fry gingerroot in oil in large skillet or wok for 1 minute. Add steak. Stir-fry for 3 minutes or until cooked through. Remove steak to bowl; keep warm. Add carrots to wok. Stir-fry for 1 minute. Add bell peppers, water chestnuts, snow peas, orange rind and cinnamon. Stir-fry for 3 minutes or until vegetables are tender-crisp. Add steak. Blend soy sauce and cornstarch in small bowl. Stir into skillet. Cook until thickened, stirring constantly. Yield: 12 servings.

Approx Per Serving: Cal 191; Prot 24 g; Carbo 11 g; Fiber 2 g;
    T Fat 6 g; Chol 54 mg; Sod 572 mg.

Dietary Exchanges: Vegetable 1 1/2; Meat 2 1/2

PEPPER STEAK

1 pound round steak, cubed
1/4 cup flour
Salt and pepper to taste
2 tablespoons oil
1 cup chopped green bell
  pepper
1 cup chopped celery

1 cup chopped onion
1   8-ounce can sliced water
  chestnuts
1   16-ounce can bean sprouts
1 tablespoon Worcestershire
  sauce
2 cups beef bouillon

Coat steak with mixture of flour, salt and pepper. Brown on all sides in oil in skillet. Add green pepper, celery, onion, water chestnuts, bean sprouts, Worcestershire sauce, bouillon, salt and pepper; mix well. Simmer for 1 1/2 hours. Serve over rice.
Yield: 6 servings.

Approx Per Serving: Cal 209; Prot 19 g; Carbo 17 g; Fiber 2 g;
    T Fat 8 g; Chol 36 mg; Sod 341 mg.

Dietary Exchanges: Vegetable 2 1/2; Bread/Starch 1/2; Meat 2; Fat 1

SAUERBRATEN

1½ pounds ½-inch thick
round steak
1 tablespoon shortening
1 envelope brown gravy mix
2 cups water
1 tablespoon onion flakes
1 tablespoon brown sugar

2 tablespoons wine vinegar
1 teaspoon Worcestershire
sauce
¼ teaspoon ginger
Salt and pepper to taste
1 bay leaf
6 cups cooked noodles

Cut steak into 1-inch squares. Brown in shortening in skillet. Remove to bowl. Stir gravy mix into pan drippings. Stir in water. Bring to a boil, stirring constantly. Add onion flakes, brown sugar, vinegar, Worcestershire sauce, ginger, salt, pepper and bay leaf; mix well. Add steak. Spoon into baking dish. Bake, covered, at 350 degrees for 1½ hours. Remove bay leaf. Serve over hot noodles. Yield: 6 servings.

Approx Per Serving: Cal 372; Prot 29 g; Carbo 43 g; Fiber 1 g;
T Fat 9 g; Chol 104 mg; Sod 259 mg.

Dietary Exchanges: Bread/Starch 2½; Meat 2½; Fat 1

SLOW COOKER BEEF BURGUNDY

6 slices bacon, chopped
4 pounds beef cubes
3 tablespoons margarine
2 4-ounce cans mushrooms,
drained
2 cloves of garlic, chopped
6 tablespoons margarine
1 cup flour

½ cup Burgundy
3 14-ounce cans beef
consommé
2 bay leaves
2 tablespoons chopped
parsley
1 teaspoon thyme
Salt and pepper to taste

Fry bacon in skillet; drain and place in slow cooker. Sear beef in skillet until brown on all sides. Add to cooker. Sauté mushrooms and garlic in 3 tablespoons margarine in skillet until mushrooms are tender. Add to cooker. Add 6 tablespoons margarine and flour to skillet; blend well. Cook until golden brown, stirring constantly. Stir in wine and consommé. Cook until thickened, stirring constantly. Add to cooker with seasonings; mix well. Cook on Medium for 7 to 8 hours. Remove bay leaves. Yield: 8 servings.

Approx Per Serving: Cal 245; Prot 8 g; Carbo 14 g; Fiber 1 g;
T Fat 16 g; Chol 12 mg; Sod 725 mg.

Dietary Exchanges: Vegetable ½; Bread/Starch 1; Meat ½; Fat 3

BRUNSWICK STEW

1½ pounds lean stew beef
2½ pounds chicken breast
  filets
1½ pounds lean pork
6 cups chopped tomatoes
4 cups chopped potatoes
2 cups butter beans
2 cups corn

1 cup chopped onion
¼ cup catsup
¼ cup vinegar
2 tablespoons
  Worcestershire sauce
1 tablespoon sugar
Salt and cayenne pepper to
  taste

Cook beef, chicken and pork in water to just cover in saucepan until tender. Drain, reserving broth. Cool and shred meat. Cook tomatoes, potatoes, beans, corn and onion in reserved broth in saucepan until tender. Add meat, catsup and remaining ingredients. Simmer for 1½ hours or to desired consistency. Chill and reheat for best flavor. Yield: 16 servings.

Approx Per Serving: Cal 324; Prot 34 g; Carbo 22 g; Fiber 3 g;
    T Fat 11 g; Chol 93 mg; Sod 273 mg.

Dietary Exchanges: Vegetable ½; Bread/Starch 1; Meat 4

BEEF AND VEGETABLE STEW

2 pounds boneless beef
  roast, trimmed
8 medium potatoes, cut into
  quarters
8 medium carrots, cut into
  quarters
1 large onion, sliced
2 cloves of garlic, minced

1 teaspoon thyme
Salt and pepper to taste
½ cup red wine
2 tablespoons melted
  margarine
2 tablespoons flour
1 cup chopped fresh parsley

Combine roast, potatoes, carrots and onion in Dutch oven. Sprinkle with garlic, thyme, salt and pepper. Drizzle with wine. Roast at 250 degrees for 4½ hours. Place roast on serving platter. Arrange vegetables around roast; keep warm. Heat pan juices in Dutch oven over high heat. Blend margarine and flour in small bowl. Stir into pan juices. Cook until thickened, stirring constantly. Spoon a small amount of gravy over roast and vegetables; sprinkle with parsley. Pour remaining gravy into bowl. Yield: 8 servings.

Approx Per Serving: Cal 378; Prot 25 g; Carbo 45 g; Fiber 6 g;
    T Fat 10 g; Chol 60 mg; Sod 123 mg.

Dietary Exchanges: Vegetable 1½; Bread/Starch 2; Meat 2½; Fat ½

HEARTY BEEF STEW

4 pounds boneless beef
  chuck, trimmed
1/2 cup flour
Salt to taste
1/4 cup oil
5 cups beef broth
1 cup dry red wine
3 tablespoons tomato paste
2 teaspoons minced garlic
2 bay leaves
2 teaspoons thyme
2 teaspoons marjoram

1 1/2 pounds carrots, cut into
  1-inch pieces
1 1/4 pounds small white
  turnips, cut into 1-inch
  wedges
2 large onions, cut into
  wedges
1 16-ounce package frozen
  cut green beans
1 pound fresh small
  mushrooms, cut into halves

Cut beef into 1 1/4-inch pieces. Coat with mixture of flour and salt, shaking to remove excess. Brown 1/3 at a time in oil in heavy saucepan, removing to bowl with slotted spoon. Drain saucepan. Return beef to saucepan. Add beef broth, wine, tomato paste, garlic, bay leaves, thyme and marjoram; mix well. Bring to a boil; reduce heat. Simmer, covered, for 1 hour. Add carrots, turnips and onions. Simmer, covered, for 45 minutes or until carrots are almost tender. Add green beans and mushrooms. Simmer, covered, for 45 minutes or until vegetables and beef are tender, stirring occasionally. Remove bay leaves. Yield: 12 servings.

Approx Per Serving: Cal 457; Prot 27 g; Carbo 19 g; Fiber 4 g;
    T Fat 29 g; Chol 82 mg; Sod 444 mg.

Dietary Exchanges: Vegetable 2 1/2; Bread/Starch 1/2; Meat 3 1/2; Fat 4

OVEN STEW

2 pounds stew beef
6 carrots, sliced
6 stalks celery, sliced
1 medium onion, sliced

Salt to taste
2 tablespoons tapioca
1 6-ounce can vegetable
  juice cocktail

Combine beef with carrots, celery and onion in 9x13-inch baking pan. Sprinkle with salt and tapioca. Drizzle with vegetable juice cocktail. Bake, tightly covered with foil, at 250 degrees for 4 hours. Yield: 6 servings.

Approx Per Serving: Cal 261; Prot 29 g; Carbo 15 g; Fiber 3 g;
    T Fat 9 g; Chol 80 mg; Sod 229 mg.

Dietary Exchanges: Vegetable 2; Meat 3 1/2

GROUND BEEF

BEEFY CABBAGE ROLLS

1 head cabbage
1 tablespoon corn oil
  margarine
1 tablespoon beef broth
1 cup grated carrots
1 cup chopped onion
1 pound lean ground round
2 cups cooked brown rice

1 tablespoon lemon juice
1 teaspoon fresh oregano
1 teaspoon fresh thyme
Salt and pepper to taste
1 28-ounce can tomatoes,
  drained, chopped
2 cups beef broth

Remove core from cabbage, leaving head intact. Place in large saucepan of boiling water. Cook, loosely covered, for 10 minutes; drain. Remove 16 outer cabbage leaves; pat dry. Melt margarine with 1 tablespoon broth in skillet over medium heat. Add carrots and onion. Sauté for 5 minutes. Add ground round, rice, lemon juice, oregano, thyme, salt and pepper. Cook for 10 minutes or until ground round is brown and crumbly, stirring frequently. Trim thick center ribs from cabbage leaves. Spoon ground round mixture onto leaves. Roll leaves to enclose filling, tucking in ends; secure with toothpicks. Arrange in 9x13-inch baking pan. Mix tomatoes with 2 cups beef broth in bowl. Pour over rolls. Bake, covered, at 375 degrees for 1 hour. Bake, uncovered, for 30 minutes longer, basting frequently. May replace foil if rolls brown too quickly. May thicken sauce with mixture of 2 tablespoons cornstarch and 2 tablespoons water if desired. Yield: 8 servings.

Approx Per Serving: Cal 210; Prot 17 g; Carbo 22 g; Fiber 4 g;
    T Fat 7 g; Chol 38 mg; Sod 418 mg.

Dietary Exchanges: Vegetable 1½; Bread/Starch 1; Meat 2; Fat ½

☎ Corn oil margarine has about two-thirds the fat content of regular margarine.

BEEFY CABBAGE WEDGE MEAL

1 small head cabbage
1 cup chopped onion
1/4 cup uncooked rice
1 pound ground beef

2 cups canned tomatoes
1 cup hot water
Salt and pepper to taste

Cut cabbage into 6 wedges. Place in buttered baking dish. Sprinkle onion and rice between wedges. Crumble ground beef between wedges. Combine tomatoes, water, salt and pepper in bowl; mix well. Pour over casserole. Bake, covered, at 350 degrees for 1½ hours. Yield: 6 servings.

Approx Per Serving: Cal 190; Prot 19 g; Carbo 14 g; Fiber 2 g;
T Fat 6 g; Chol 51 mg; Sod 176 mg.

Dietary Exchanges: Vegetable 1½; Bread/Starch ½; Meat 2½

DOLMAS

1 pound ground beef
1 onion, finely chopped
2 cloves of garlic, chopped
1/2 cup uncooked rice
2 teaspoons mint flakes
1 teaspoon parsley flakes

Salt and pepper to taste
24 grape leaves
1 10-ounce can condensed
  chicken broth
2 eggs
Juice of 1½ lemons

Combine ground beef, onion, garlic, rice, mint flakes, parsley flakes, salt and pepper in bowl; mix well. Spoon onto grape leaves; roll to enclose filling. Place in pressure cooker. Add chicken broth. Cook at 15 pounds pressure for 10 minutes, following manufacturer's instructions. Cool pressure cooker by partially submerging in cold water. Beat eggs in small bowl. Beat in lemon juice gradually. Stir in broth from pressure cooker gradually. Pour over dolmas in serving bowl. May purchase grape leaves in jars in specialty section of most food markets. May substitute cabbage leaves for grape leaves. Yield: 4 servings.

Approx Per Serving: Cal 346; Prot 33 g; Carbo 24 g; Fiber 1 g;
T Fat 12 g; Chol 213 mg; Sod 336 mg.
Nutritional information does not include grape leaves.

Dietary Exchanges: Vegetable ½; Bread/Starch 1; Meat 4; Fat ½

PIZZA CASSEROLE

1 pound ground beef
1½ cups chopped onions
1½ cups macaroni, cooked, drained
1 15-ounce can tomato sauce with tomato bits

¼ cup water
½ teaspoon basil
¼ teaspoon oregano
½ teaspoon garlic powder
2 cups shredded mozzarella cheese

Brown ground beef with onions in skillet, stirring until ground beef is crumbly; drain. Add macaroni, tomato sauce, water, basil, oregano and garlic powder; mix well. Layer ground beef mixture and cheese ½ at a time in 2-quart baking dish. Bake at 375 degrees for 20 minutes or until heated through. Yield: 6 servings.

Approx Per Serving: Cal 376; Prot 30 g; Carbo 31 g; Fiber 2 g;
    T Fat 15 g; Chol 80 mg; Sod 610 mg.

Dietary Exchanges: Vegetable 1½; Bread/Starch 1½; Meat 3½; Fat ½

BEEF AND VEGETABLE CASSEROLE

12 ounces ground beef
½ cup uncooked rice
2 potatoes, thinly sliced

1 onion, thinly sliced
1 green bell pepper, sliced
1 8-ounce can tomatoes

Brown ground beef in skillet, stirring until crumbly; drain. Layer ground beef, rice, potatoes, onion, green pepper and tomatoes in baking dish. Bake at 350 degrees for 1½ hours or until rice and vegetables are tender. Yield: 4 servings.

Approx Per Serving: Cal 329; Prot 24 g; Carbo 42 g; Fiber 3 g;
    T Fat 7 g; Chol 57 mg; Sod 141 mg.

Dietary Exchanges: Vegetable 1; Bread/Starch 2; Meat 2½

☎ Look for the reduced-sodium and no-salt-added lines of vegetable and tomato products in your supermarket to reduce sodium in your diet.

THREE-ALARM CHILI

1 pound lean ground beef
1 medium onion, finely
  chopped
3 cloves of garlic, minced
1 large green bell pepper,
  chopped
2 28-ounce cans tomatoes,
  crushed
1 tablespoon oil
2 teaspoons oregano

2 teaspoons cumin
3 tablespoons chili powder
2 tablespoons baking cocoa
2 teaspoons sugar
1 teaspoon crushed hot
  pepper
1 teaspoon Tabasco sauce
1 15-ounce can kidney
  beans, rinsed, drained

Brown ground beef in 2½-quart saucepan over medium heat for 6 to 8 minutes, stirring until crumbly. Drain ground beef and saucepan. Sauté onion, garlic and green pepper with ½ cup tomatoes in oil in saucepan for 3 minutes. Add oregano, cumin, chili powder, cocoa, sugar, hot pepper and Tabasco sauce. Cook for 3 minutes. Add beans, ground beef and remaining tomatoes. Simmer for 25 minutes. Yield: 8 servings.

Approx Per Serving: Cal 223; Prot 19 g; Carbo 23 g; Fiber 5 g;
    T Fat 8 g; Chol 38 mg; Sod 554 mg.

Dietary Exchanges: Vegetable 2; Bread/Starch 1; Meat 2; Fat ½

MEATBALLS WITH SAUCE

1 pound ground beef
½ cup oats
½ cup evaporated milk
Salt and pepper to taste
½ cup chopped green bell
  pepper
½ cup chopped onion

2 tablespoons steak sauce
½ cup catsup
½ cup water
1½ tablespoons
  Worcestershire sauce
3 tablespoons sugar

Combine ground beef, oats, evaporated milk, salt and pepper in bowl; mix well. Shape into balls; place in deep baking dish. Combine green pepper, onion, steak sauce, catsup, water, Worcestershire sauce and sugar in bowl; mix well. Pour over meatballs. Bake at 350 degrees for 1 hour. Yield: 6 servings.

Approx Per Serving: Cal 232; Prot 20 g; Carbo 20 g; Fiber 1 g;
    T Fat 8 g; Chol 57 mg; Sod 305 mg.

Dietary Exchanges: Vegetable ½; Bread/Starch ½; Meat 2½; Fat ½

BARBECUED MEAT LOAF

1½ pounds lean ground
   chuck
½ cup oats
¼ cup unprocessed oat bran
½ cup chopped onion
¼ cup chopped green bell
   pepper
⅓ cup barbecue sauce
¼ cup egg substitute
2 tablespoons parsley flakes
2 tablespoons reduced-
   sodium Worcestershire
   sauce
¼ teaspoon pepper

Combine ground chuck, oats, oat bran, onion, green pepper, barbecue sauce, egg substitute, parsley flakes, Worcestershire sauce and pepper in bowl; mix well. Shape into loaf. Spray nonstick cooking spray over bottom and sides of 2-piece 5x9-inch loaf pan with drain rack in bottom. Place meat loaf in pan. Bake at 350 degrees for 1 hour. Remove to serving plate; let stand for 5 to 10 minutes before serving. Yield: 8 servings.

Approx Per Serving: Cal 192; Prot 22 g; Carbo 11 g; Fiber 1 g;
   T Fat 7 g; Chol 57 mg; Sod 68 mg.

Dietary Exchanges: Bread/Starch ½; Meat 2½

CURRIED MEAT LOAF

2 small sweet apples
½ cup chopped onion
4 teaspoons margarine
1 pound ground beef
2 teaspoons curry powder
⅛ teaspoon garlic powder
2 egg whites
½ cup wheat germ
Salt and pepper to taste
¾ cup tomato sauce
2 tablespoons brown sugar

Sauté apples and onion in margarine in saucepan until light brown. Add ground beef, curry powder, garlic powder, egg whites, wheat germ, salt, pepper and half the tomato sauce; mix well. Shape into loaf; place in baking pan. Top with remaining tomato sauce and brown sugar. Bake at 350 degrees for 1 hour. Yield: 6 servings.

Approx Per Serving: Cal 250; Prot 22 g; Carbo 20 g; Fiber 2 g;
   T Fat 10 g; Chol 51 mg; Sod 271 mg.

Dietary Exchanges: Vegetable ½; Fruit ½; Bread/Starch ½; Meat 2½; Fat 1

COMPANY MEAT LOAF

2 pounds ground round
1 cup fresh bread crumbs
1 large onion, chopped
1 egg, beaten
1/2 cup milk
Salt and pepper to taste

1 6-ounce can tomato paste
2 tablespoons mustard
2 tablespoons vinegar
2 tablespoons brown sugar
1/4 cup water

Combine ground round, bread crumbs, onion, egg, milk, salt, pepper and half the tomato paste in bowl; mix well. Press into baking dish. Bake at 350 degrees for 40 minutes; drain. Combine remaining tomato paste, mustard, vinegar, brown sugar and water in bowl; mix well. Spoon over meat loaf. Bake for 35 minutes longer, basting occasionally. Yield: 8 servings.

Approx Per Serving: Cal 238; Prot 30 g; Carbo 13 g; Fiber <1 g;
T Fat 7 g; Chol 105 mg; Sod 166 mg.

Dietary Exchanges: Vegetable 1; Meat 3 1/2; Fat 1/2

ORIENTAL MEAT LOAF

1 pound lean ground beef
3/4 cup whole wheat bread
  crumbs
1/4 cup finely chopped onion
1/4 cup finely chopped green
  bell pepper

1/4 cup chopped water
  chestnuts
1/4 cup catsup
1 egg, beaten
1 1/2 tablespoons soy sauce
1/4 teaspoon pepper

Combine ground beef, bread crumbs, onion, green pepper, water chestnuts, catsup, egg, soy sauce and pepper in bowl; mix well. Shape into round loaf. Place in ridged microwave plate sprayed with nonstick cooking spray. Microwave, covered with heavy-duty plastic wrap, on High for 10 to 14 minutes or until cooked through, turning plate after 5 minutes. Drain well. Let stand for 5 minutes. Yield: 4 servings.

Approx Per Serving: Cal 263; Prot 29 g; Carbo 12 g; Fiber 1 g;
T Fat 11 g; Chol 145 mg; Sod 682 mg.

Dietary Exchanges: Vegetable 1/2; Bread/Starch 1/2; Meat 4; Fat 1/2

ZESTY MEAT LOAF

1¹/2 pounds lean ground beef
4 ounces ground pork
¹/4 cup chopped onion
¹/4 cup catsup
1 cup oats

1 teaspoon mustard
1 egg, beaten
1 cup milk
Salt and pepper to taste
¹/2 cup catsup

Combine ground beef, ground pork, onion, ¹/4 cup catsup, oats, mustard, egg, milk, salt and pepper in bowl; mix well. Press into 8x12-inch baking dish. Spread remaining ¹/2 cup catsup over top. Bake at 375 degrees for 1 hour; drain. Yield: 8 servings.

Approx Per Serving: Cal 261; Prot 26 g; Carbo 15 g; Fiber 1 g;
T Fat 11 g; Chol 106 mg; Sod 315 mg.

Dietary Exchanges: Bread/Starch ¹/2; Meat 3; Fat ¹/2

LASAGNA FLORENTINE

1 pound lean ground beef
1 medium onion, chopped
¹/4 cup chopped celery
¹/4 cup chopped green bell
   pepper
2 cloves of garlic, minced
1¹/2 cups tomato purée
1 teaspoon oregano
1 teaspoon basil

Salt and pepper to taste
2 10-ounce packages frozen
   chopped spinach, thawed
1¹/2 cups low-fat cottage
   cheese
1 egg, beaten
3 tablespoons Parmesan
   cheese
¹/8 teaspoon nutmeg

Brown ground beef in large nonstick skillet, stirring until crumbly. Remove ground beef with slotted spoon. Drain skillet, reserving 1 teaspoon drippings. Add onion, celery and green pepper to drippings in skillet. Sauté until tender. Add garlic. Sauté for 1 minute. Add beef, tomato purée, oregano, basil, salt and pepper. Heat until bubbly; reduce heat. Simmer for 5 minutes. Combine spinach, cottage cheese, egg, Parmesan cheese, nutmeg, salt and pepper in bowl; mix well. Layer spinach mixture and ground beef mixture ¹/3 at a time in lightly greased 9x9-inch baking pan. Bake, covered with foil, at 350 degrees for 40 to 45 minutes or until heated through. Yield: 6 servings.

Approx Per Serving: Cal 258; Prot 31 g; Carbo 16 g; Fiber 3 g;
T Fat 9 g; Chol 101 mg; Sod 435 mg.

Dietary Exchanges: Vegetable 2¹/2; Meat 3¹/2

ZUCCHINI LASAGNA

8 ounces lean ground beef
1/2 cup chopped onion
1   15-ounce can tomato
   sauce
1/2 teaspoon oregano
1/4 teaspoon basil
Salt and pepper to taste

4 medium zucchini
8 ounces cottage cheese
1 egg
2 tablespoons flour
1 cup shredded low-fat
   mozzarella cheese

Brown ground beef with onion in skillet, stirring until ground beef is crumbly; drain. Stir in tomato sauce, oregano, basil, salt and pepper. Simmer for 5 minutes. Slice zucchini lengthwise 1/4 inch thick. Combine cottage cheese and egg in bowl; mix well. Arrange half the zucchini slices in 8x12-inch baking dish. Sprinkle with half the flour. Layer cottage cheese mixture, half the ground beef mixture, remaining zucchini, remaining flour, mozzarella cheese and remaining ground beef in pan. Bake at 375 degrees for 40 minutes. Let stand for 10 minutes. Yield: 6 servings.

Approx Per Serving: Cal 214; Prot 21 g; Carbo 12 g; Fiber 2 g;
   T Fat 9 g; Chol 87 mg; Sod 609 mg.

Dietary Exchanges: Vegetable 1 1/2; Meat 3; Fat 1/2

POTATO AND GROUND BEEF SKILLET

1 pound ground beef
1 large onion, sliced
1 teaspoon parsley flakes
1 teaspoon dried mint

Salt and pepper to taste
1   16-ounce can tomatoes
4 large potatoes, peeled,
   sliced 1/4 inch thick

Brown ground beef in saucepan, stirring until crumbly; drain. Add onion, parsley flakes, mint, salt and pepper; mix well. Sauté for 5 minutes or until onion is tender-crisp. Stir in tomatoes. Simmer for 10 minutes. Alternate layers of ground beef mixture and potatoes in large skillet, beginning and ending with ground beef. Cover skillet. Cook until bubbling; reduce heat very low. Simmer for 45 minutes to 1 hour or until potatoes are tender. Let stand for 10 minutes. May substitute yellow squash or zucchini for potatoes. May bake, covered, at 375 degrees for 1 hour if preferred. Yield: 6 servings.

Approx Per Serving: Cal 229; Prot 20 g; Carbo 23 g; Fiber 2 g;
   T Fat 6 g; Chol 51 mg; Sod 164 mg.

Dietary Exchanges: Vegetable 1; Bread/Starch 1; Meat 2 1/2

MOUSSAKA

1 pound ground chuck
1 pound ground veal
1 cup chopped onion
1 clove of garlic, crushed
1   16-ounce can tomato
   sauce
1/2 teaspoon oregano
1 teaspoon basil

1/2 teaspoon cinnamon
Salt and pepper to taste
2   1-pound eggplant, peeled
3 tablespoons cornstarch
2 cups skim milk
2 eggs, beaten
1/2 cup Parmesan cheese

Brown ground chuck and veal with onion and garlic in heavy saucepan, stirring until crumbly; drain. Add tomato sauce and seasonings. Simmer for 30 minutes. Slice eggplant 1/4 inch thick. Place in shallow dish. Pour boiling water over top. Let stand for 5 minutes. Drain and pat dry. Mix cornstarch, salt and pepper in small saucepan. Stir in milk gradually. Cook until thickened, stirring constantly. Stir a small amount of hot mixture into eggs; stir eggs into hot mixture. Layer half the eggplant, meat sauce, half the cheeses, remaining eggplant, cream sauce and remaining cheese in baking dish. Bake at 350 degrees for 35 minutes or until brown. Let stand for 10 minutes. Yield: 8 servings.

Approx Per Serving: Cal 402; Prot 30 g; Carbo 19 g; Fiber 4 g;
    T Fat 22 g; Chol 157 mg; Sod 496 mg.

Dietary Exchanges: Milk 1/2; Vegetable 21/2; Meat 4; Fat 2

STUFFED PEPPERS

8 medium green bell peppers
1 pound lean ground round
11/2 cups cooked brown rice
1 egg, beaten
1/2 cup grated carrots
2 teaspoons fresh oregano

Salt and pepper to taste
2 cups chopped fresh
   tomatoes
1 cup tomato sauce
1/2 cup finely chopped onion
1 tablespoon lemon juice

Cut peppers into halves lengthwise, discarding seed. Combine ground round, rice, egg, carrots, oregano, salt and pepper in bowl; mix well. Spoon into pepper shells; arrange in large baking dish. Mix remaining ingredients in bowl. Spoon over and around peppers. Bake, covered with foil, at 350 degrees for 1 hour. Yield: 8 servings.

Approx Per Serving: Cal 188; Prot 16 g; Carbo 18 g; Fiber 3 g
    T Fat 6 g; Chol 72 mg; Sod 228 mg.

Dietary Exchanges: Vegetable 1/2; Bread/Starch 1/2; Meat 2

VEAL

VEAL-STUFFED ARTICHOKES

6 French (globe) artichokes
2 quarts water
1/4 cup minced onion
2 tablespoons margarine
1/4 cup Port
1 1/2 pounds ground veal
1 egg, slightly beaten
1/4 teaspoon allspice
1/2 teaspoon thyme
1 clove of garlic, crushed

Salt and pepper to taste
3 tablespoons flour
2 tablespoons melted
  margarine
2 cups water
1 28-ounce can tomatoes,
  puréed
1 6-ounce can tomato paste
Parsley, chervil, tarragon and
  basil to taste

Cut stems and small leaves from bases of artichokes; trim points of leaves with scissors. Rinse artichokes. Bring 2 quarts water to a boil in stockpot. Add artichokes. Boil for 35 to 45 minutes or until leaf pulls out easily. Remove and drain upside down on towel; cool slightly. Spread leaves apart to reach interior of artichoke. Remove center cone of leaves in 1 piece; set aside. Scrape, remove and discard the choke from heart. Sauté onion in 2 tablespoons margarine in skillet just until tender; do not brown. Remove to small bowl. Add wine to skillet, stirring to deglaze. Cook until wine is reduced by half. Pour over onion. Combine veal, egg, allspice, thyme, garlic, salt and pepper in bowl; beat until well mixed and light in texture. Add sautéed onion and wine; mix well. Sauté in skillet until veal is cooked through. Spoon into artichokes. Replace center cones. Press leaves back into place; secure with string. Blend flour with 2 tablespoons melted margarine in saucepan over low heat. Cook for 2 minutes, stirring constantly. Whisk in 2 cups water. Cook until thickened, stirring constantly. Add tomatoes, tomato paste, parsley, chervil, tarragon, basil, salt and pepper; mix well. Pour into stockpot; add artichokes. Cook, covered, over low heat until heated through. Serve immediately. Spoon sauce over tops of artichokes.
Yield: 6 servings.

Approx Per Serving: Cal 438; Prot 30 g; Carbo 27 g; Fiber 5 g;
    T Fat 23 g; Chol 133 mg; Sod 487 mg.

Dietary Exchanges: Vegetable 4; Meat 3 1/2; Fat 3

VEAL PICCATA

8 2-ounce veal cutlets
1/2 cup flour
Salt and pepper to taste
1/4 cup margarine
Juice of 1 lemon

1/4 cup dry white wine
2 tablespoons capers
2 tablespoons margarine
1 lemon, sliced

Pound veal with meat mallet to flatten. Coat with mixture of flour, salt and pepper, shaking off excess. Brown in 1/4 cup margarine in large skillet over medium heat for 2 minutes on each side. Remove to warm platter. Add lemon juice and wine to skillet, stirring to deglaze. Add capers. Add 2 tablespoons margarine, stirring until melted; remove from heat. Pour over veal. Top with lemon slices. Yield: 4 servings.

Approx Per Serving: Cal 407; Prot 20 g; Carbo 15 g; Fiber <1 g;
   T Fat 28 g; Chol 68 mg; Sod 261 mg.

Dietary Exchanges: Fruit 1/2; Bread/Starch 1; Meat 2 1/2; Fat 4 1/2

VEAL SCALLOPINI DIJON

1 1/2 pounds veal scallopini
1 teaspoon freshly ground
   pepper
1 tablespoon olive oil
4 cloves of garlic, minced
1 tablespoon margarine
2 tablespoons dry white wine
2 tablespoons chicken broth

1 tablespoon Dijon mustard
1/2 teaspoon basil
1/4 teaspoon each thyme,
   dillweed, celery seed,
   onion powder and parsley
   flakes
1/4 cup chopped fresh parsley

Pound veal with meat mallet to flatten; sprinkle with pepper. Brown in olive oil in skillet for 30 seconds on each side. Remove to warm platter; wipe pan. Sauté garlic in margarine in skillet for 30 seconds. Add wine, chicken broth, mustard, basil, thyme, dillweed, celery seed, onion powder and parsley flakes; mix well. Add veal; sprinkle with fresh parsley. Cook for 1 minute longer or until heated through. Yield: 6 servings.

Approx Per Serving: Cal 228; Prot 18 g; Carbo 1 g; Fiber <1 g;
   T Fat 15 g; Chol 69 mg; Sod 129 mg.

Dietary Exchanges: Meat 2 1/2; Fat 1 1/2

PORK

BARBECUED PORK CHOPS

6 pork chops, trimmed
2 tablespoons oil
1 medium onion, chopped
3 cloves of garlic, minced
1 6-ounce can tomato paste
1/2 cup cider vinegar
6 tablespoons brown sugar

1/4 cup water
3 tablespoons
   Worcestershire sauce
1 teaspoon dry mustard
1 teaspoon chili powder
1/4 teaspoon salt
1/4 teaspoon pepper

Brown pork chops lightly in oil in large skillet over medium-high heat. Arrange in single layer in 9x13-inch baking dish. Add onion and garlic to drippings in skillet. Sauté until tender. Add remaining ingredients; mix well. Simmer for 5 minutes. Pour over pork chops, turning chops to coat well. Bake at 350 degrees for 45 to 60 minutes or until tender. Yield: 6 servings.

Approx Per Serving: Cal 386; Prot 29 g; Carbo 24 g; Fiber <1 g;
   T Fat 20 g; Chol 95 mg; Sod 253 mg.

Dietary Exchanges: Vegetable 1 1/2; Meat 4 1/2; Fat 1

BARBECUED PORK LOIN

1 5-pound pork loin
1/2 cup chopped onion
1 tablespoon oil
3/4 cup water
3/4 cup catsup
1/2 cup cider vinegar
3 tablespoons brown sugar

4 teaspoons Worcestershire
   sauce
3/4 teaspoon each oregano,
   paprika and garlic powder
1/4 teaspoon dry mustard
Cloves, salt and pepper to
   taste

Place pork loin on rack in shallow roasting pan. Roast at 325 degrees for 3 hours. Sauté onion in oil in saucepan. Add remaining ingredients; mix well. Brush over pork. Roast for 30 minutes longer or to 170 degrees on meat thermometer, brushing several times with sauce. Serve with remaining sauce. Yield: 10 servings.

Approx Per Serving: Cal 401; Prot 42 g; Carbo 11 g; Fiber <1 g;
   T Fat 21 g; Chol 133 mg; Sod 310 mg.

Dietary Exchanges: Meat 6; Fat 1/2

BARBECUED LIMA BEANS AND HAM

1½ cups dried large lima
  beans
5 cups water
Salt to taste
1 cup chopped cooked ham
1 medium onion, sliced

½ cup catsup
1 tablespoon Worcestershire
  sauce
¼ teaspoon chili powder
Pepper sauce to taste

    Bring beans, water and salt to a boil in saucepan; remove from heat. Let stand for several hours. Bring to a boil; reduce heat. Simmer, covered, for 1 hour. Drain, reserving ½ cup liquid. Layer beans, ham and onion in 2-quart bean pot. Combine reserved liquid with catsup, Worcestershire sauce, chili powder, pepper sauce and salt in bowl; mix well. Pour over beans. Bake, covered, at 350 degrees for 1 hour or until beans are tender. Yield: 8 servings.

Approx Per Serving: Cal 169; Prot 12 g; Carbo 26 g; Fiber 8 g;
    T Fat 2 g; Chol 10 mg; Sod 446 mg.

Dietary Exchanges: Vegetable ½; Bread/Starch 1½; Meat 1

HAM AND CHEESE QUICHE

3 eggs, beaten
¾ cup milk
Salt and pepper to taste
1 cup chopped cooked ham

1 cup shredded sharp
  Cheddar cheese
1 unbaked 9-inch pie shell

    Beat eggs with milk, salt and pepper in bowl. Add ham and cheese. Pour into pie shell. Bake at 350 degrees for 45 minutes. Let stand for several minutes. Yield: 6 servings.

Approx Per Serving: Cal 326; Prot 16 g; Carbo 15 g; Fiber 0 g;
    T Fat 22 g; Chol 175 mg; Sod 700 mg.

Dietary Exchanges: Bread/Starch 1; Meat 2; Fat 3½

1919

LAMB

EASY CURRIED LAMB

2 cups chopped onions
2 tablespoons oil
1 pound lean lamb, cubed

1 cup plain low-fat yogurt
2 tablespoons curry powder

Brown onions in oil in heavy skillet. Remove onions with slotted spoon; drain. Brown lamb on all sides in drippings in skillet. Add onions, yogurt and curry powder; mix well. Simmer, covered, for 1 hour or until lamb is tender, adding water if needed for desired consistency. Serve with rice. May serve with bowls of condiments such as mango chutney, bananas, peanuts and scallions. Yield: 5 servings.

Approx Per Serving: Cal 224; Prot 19 g; Carbo 9 g; Fiber 1 g;
T Fat 13 g; Chol 58 mg; Sod 73 mg.

Dietary Exchanges: Milk 1/2; Vegetable 1; Meat 2; Fat 1

LEG OF LAMB WITH ARTICHOKES

1 5-pound leg of lamb, boned
1 clove of garlic
Juice of 1 lemon
1 clove of garlic, slivered
1 teaspoon oregano
Salt and pepper to taste

**2 8-ounce cans tomato
    sauce**
1 cup water
1 lemon, sliced
**2 16-ounce cans artichoke
    hearts, drained**

Rub cut edges of lamb with 1 clove of garlic; sprinkle with lemon juice. Roll lamb; tie at 1 1/2-inch intervals. Cut slits in lamb; insert garlic slivers. Rub with remaining lemon juice, oregano, salt and pepper. Place in roasting pan. Roast at 400 degrees for 30 minutes. Reduce oven temperature to 350 degrees. Roast lamb to 130 degrees on meat thermometer, basting frequently with pan drippings. Skim drippings. Add tomato sauce, water and lemon slices; mix well. Roast for 15 minutes. Add artichoke hearts. Roast for 15 minutes or to 150 to 160 degrees on meat thermometer for medium, basting frequently. Place lamb on heated platter. Arrange artichoke hearts around lamb. Strain sauce; serve with lamb. Yield: 10 servings.

Approx Per Serving: Cal 315; Prot 42 g; Carbo 14 g; Fiber 3 g;
T Fat 10 g; Chol 133 mg; Sod 431 mg.

Dietary Exchanges: Vegetable 2 1/2; Meat 5

SPANISH LAMB STEW

1 pound lean lamb cubes
1 tablespoon olive oil
1 cup dry red wine
1 cup chopped tomatoes
1 large onion, sliced
1 green bell pepper, cut into
  strips
1/4 cup golden raisins
1/4 cup chopped dried apricots

1 clove of garlic, minced
1/8 teaspoon pepper
1 teaspoon each basil, thyme
  and tarragon
1 bay leaf
1/2 cup sliced mushrooms
1/4 cup sliced black olives
1 tablespoon flour
1 cup cold water

Brown lamb in olive oil in large saucepan. Add wine, tomatoes, onion, green pepper, raisins, apricots, garlic and seasonings; mix well. Simmer, covered, for 1 hour. Add mushrooms and olives. Simmer for 30 minutes longer. Blend flour and water in small bowl. Stir into stew. Cook until thickened, stirring constantly. Remove bay leaf. Serve over brown rice or couscous. Yield: 6 servings.

Approx Per Serving: Cal 220; Prot 15 g; Carbo 15 g; Fiber 2 g;
    T Fat 10 g; Chol 46 mg; Sod 186 mg.

Dietary Exchanges: Vegetable 1; Fruit 1/2; Meat 2; Fat 1

VENISON STEW

2 pounds venison cubes
1 clove of garlic, chopped
2 tablespoons oil
1 teaspoon Worcestershire
  sauce
1 teaspoon lemon juice
1 small bay leaf
Salt and pepper to taste

4 cups hot water
3 medium potatoes, chopped
4 carrots, sliced
1 cup sliced celery
2 cups cooked green peas
1/4 cup flour
1/2 cup water

Brown venison with garlic in oil in stockpot. Add Worcestershire sauce, lemon juice, bay leaf, salt, pepper and 2 cups hot water; mix well. Simmer, covered, for 2 hours, stirring occasionally. Remove bay leaf. Add remaining 2 cups hot water, potatoes, carrots and celery; mix well. Simmer for 30 minutes, stirring frequently. Add peas. Blend flour with 1/2 cup water. Add to stew. Cook until thickened, stirring constantly. Yield: 8 servings.

Approx Per Serving: Cal 245; Prot 24 g; Carbo 25 g; Fiber 4 g;
    T Fat 5 g; Chol 0 mg; Sod 175 mg.

Dietary Exchanges: Vegetable 1/2; Bread/Starch 1 1/2; Meat 2; Fat 1/2

VEGETABLE CHILI

1 large onion, chopped
1 tablespoon olive oil
1 28-ounce can whole
  tomatoes
2/3 cup picante sauce
1 1/2 teaspoons chili powder
1 1/2 teaspoons cumin

3/4 teaspoon salt
1 16-ounce can pinto beans,
  drained
1 large zucchini, chopped
1 cup whole kernel corn
1/8 teaspoon cayenne pepper

Sauté onion in olive oil in heavy saucepan for 2 to 3 minutes. Add tomatoes, picante sauce, chili powder, cumin and salt. Simmer, covered, for 10 minutes. Add beans, zucchini, corn and cayenne pepper. Simmer, covered, for 10 minutes. Serve with additional picante sauce. Yield: 6 servings.

Approx Per Serving: Cal 214; Prot 10 g; Carbo 39 g; Fiber 6 g;
    T Fat 4 g; Chol 0 mg; Sod 731 mg.

Dietary Exchanges: Vegetable 1 1/2; Bread/Starch 2; Fat 1/2

VEGETARIAN CHILI WITH RICE

1 16-ounce can red kidney
  beans, drained
1 16-ounce can Great
  Northern beans, drained
1 15-ounce can tomatoes,
  chopped
1 8-ounce can tomato sauce
3/4 cup chopped green bell
  pepper

1/2 cup chopped onion
1 cup water
1 tablespoon chili powder
1 teaspoon sugar
1/2 teaspoon basil
2 cloves of garlic, minced
2 cups hot cooked rice

Combine kidney beans, Great Northern beans, undrained tomatoes, tomato sauce, green pepper, onion, water, chili powder, sugar, basil and garlic; mix well. Bring to a boil; reduce heat. Simmer, covered, for 15 minutes, stirring occasionally. Spoon into serving bowls. Top with rice. Yield: 4 servings.

Approx Per Serving: Cal 415; Prot 21 g; Carbo 82 g; Fiber 13 g;
    T Fat 2 g; Chol 0 mg; Sod 911 mg.

Dietary Exchanges: Vegetable 2; Bread/Starch 5

ZUCCHINI QUICHE

1 unbaked 9-inch pie shell
3 eggs, beaten
1 cup plain low-fat yogurt
1½ cups shredded Swiss
   cheese
2 tablespoons flour

½ teaspoon dillweed
Salt and pepper to taste
2 cups finely chopped
   zucchini
1 medium onion, finely
   chopped

Bake pie shell at 450 degrees for 5 to 7 minutes or until edge is light brown. Combine next 6 ingredients in mixer bowl; beat until smooth. Stir in zucchini and onion. Pour into hot pie shell. Reduce oven temperature to 350 degrees. Bake for 25 to 30 minutes or until set. Let stand for 10 minutes. Yield: 6 servings.

Approx Per Serving: Cal 335; Prot 15 g; Carbo 22 g; Fiber 1 g;
   T Fat 21 g; Chol 164 mg; Sod 639 mg.

Dietary Exchanges: Milk ½; Vegetable ½; Bread/Starch 1; Meat 1½; Fat 3½

STEAMED VEGETABLES OVER RICE

1 cup uncooked brown rice
1¾ cups water
8 new potatoes
2 carrots, cut into halves
1 medium onion, cut into
   quarters

Flowerets of 1 bunch broccoli
2 small yellow squash, cut
   into halves
20 tender young green beans
10 asparagus spears

Cook rice in water using package directions. Peel 1 strip around center of potatoes. Layer carrots, potatoes, onion, broccoli, squash, green beans and asparagus in that order in steamer basket. Place in large stockpot with water up to but not covering basket. Steam vegetables for 10 minutes or until tender-crisp. Serve over rice. Serve with Dijon Yogurt (page 127) or Oriental Sauce (below). Yield: 4 servings.

Approx Per Serving: Cal 417; Prot 13 g; Carbo 91 g; Fiber 14 g;
   T Fat 2 g; Chol 0 mg; Sod 278 mg.

Dietary Exchanges: Vegetable 4½; Bread/Starch 4½

☎ Serve **Oriental Sauce** warm over vegetables and rice. Cook 1 cup water, 2 tablespoons cornstarch and 2 tablespoons soy sauce in small saucepan until thickened, stirring constantly.

HERBED SPINACH PASTA

1/2 medium onion, sliced
1 clove of garlic, minced
2 teaspoons olive oil
2 ounces uncooked rotini
3/4 teaspoon *fines herbs*
1 cup water
1/2 medium red or green bell
  pepper, cut into strips

1 15-ounce can whole leaf
   spinach, well drained
1 tablespoon lemon juice
2 tablespoons Parmesan
   cheese

Sauté onion and garlic in olive oil in skillet until tender. Add pasta, *fines herbs* and water. Bring to a boil; reduce heat. Simmer, covered, for 5 minutes. Add bell pepper. Cook for 5 minutes. Stir in spinach and lemon juice. Cook until heated through. Spoon into serving bowl. Top with cheese. Yield: 2 servings.

Approx Per Serving: Cal 246; Prot 12 g; Carbo 34 g; Fiber 9 g;
    T Fat 8 g; Chol 5 mg; Sod 175 mg.

Dietary Exchanges: Vegetable 2; Bread/Starch 2; Meat 1/2; Fat 1/2

PASTA WITH MARINARA SAUCE

1 cup chopped onion
1 tablespoon olive oil
6 cloves of garlic, minced
1 teaspoon oregano
1/2 teaspoon thyme
1/2 teaspoon crushed fennel
1 teaspoon basil
2 tablespoons chopped parsley

1/4 teaspoon pepper
2 28-ounce cans whole
   tomatoes, chopped
1 8-ounce can tomato sauce
2 bay leaves
1/2 cup wine
16 ounces pasta, cooked

Sauté onion in olive oil in saucepan until tender. Add garlic, oregano, thyme, fennel, basil, parsley and pepper. Cook for 1 minute, stirring constantly. Add tomatoes, tomato sauce and bay leaves. Bring to a boil; reduce heat. Add wine. Simmer for 30 minutes. Remove bay leaves. Serve over pasta. Yield: 10 servings.

Approx Per Serving: Cal 236; Prot 8 g; Carbo 45 g; Fiber 4 g;
    T Fat 2 g; Chol 0 mg; Sod 405 mg.

Dietary Exchanges: Vegetable 2; Bread/Starch 2 1/2; Fat 1/2

TOFU LASAGNA

8 whole wheat lasagna
  noodles, cooked
2 cups Ratatouille (page 133)
1½ cups ricotta cheese
1½ cups tofu

1 cup shredded Cheddar
  cheese
2 eggs
½ cup yogurt

Layer half the noodles in greased 9x9-inch baking dish. Top with ratatouille. Mash ricotta cheese and tofu in bowl. Spread half the mixture over ratatouille. Sprinkle with half the Cheddar cheese. Layer remaining noodles and tofu mixture in dish. Beat eggs with yogurt in small bowl. Pour over layers. Top with remaining Cheddar cheese. Bake at 350 degrees for 30 minutes. Yield: 8 servings.

Approx Per Serving: Cal 350; Prot 22 g; Carbo 28 g; Fiber 1 g;
    T Fat 18 g; Chol 108 mg; Sod 473 mg.

Dietary Exchanges: Vegetable 1; Bread/Starch 1½; Meat 2; Fat 2½

MICROWAVE VEGETARIAN LASAGNA

2 10-ounce packages frozen
  chopped spinach
8 ounces tofu
8 ounces low-fat cottage
  cheese
¼ cup Parmesan cheese
1 32-ounce jar meatless
  spaghetti sauce

½ cup dry red wine
¼ teaspoon garlic powder
⅛ teaspoon nutmeg
8 uncooked lasagna noodles
8 ounces mozzarella cheese,
  sliced
1 cup sliced fresh mushrooms

Microwave spinach on High in 2-quart glass dish for 5 to 6 minutes or until tender. Drain well. Crumble tofu into bowl. Stir in cottage cheese and Parmesan cheese. Combine spaghetti sauce, wine, garlic powder and nutmeg in 2-quart glass dish. Microwave, covered, on High for 6 to 8 minutes or until heated through. Reserve 1 cup sauce. Add spinach to remaining sauce; mix well. Layer spinach mixture, noodles, cottage cheese mixture, mozzarella cheese and mushrooms ½ at a time in rectangular 2-quart glass dish. Top with reserved sauce. Microwave, covered with plastic wrap, on High for 6 minutes. Rotate dish. Microwave on Medium-High for 20 minutes. Let stand for 12 minutes before serving. Yield: 8 servings.

Approx Per Serving: Cal 424; Prot 24 g; Carbo 47 g; Fiber 2 g;
    T Fat 16 g; Chol 27 mg; Sod 920 mg.

Dietary Exchanges: Vegetable 4; Bread/Starch 1½; Meat 2½; Fat 2

LIGHT SPAGHETTI PRIMAVERA

1/2 cup low-calorie Italian
   salad dressing
1 green bell pepper, chopped
1 red bell pepper, chopped
1 yellow squash, cut into
   julienne strips
1 cup sliced fresh mushrooms
1/4 cup chopped onion

1/4 cup sliced black olives
1 8-ounce package thin
   spaghetti, cooked
1/4 cup shredded mozzarella
   cheese
3 tablespoons chopped fresh
   parsley

Combine salad dressing and vegetables in preheated skillet. Stir-fry until vegetables are tender-crisp. Stir in olives. Spoon over hot cooked spaghetti on serving platter. Sprinkle cheese and parsley over top. Yield: 4 servings.

Approx Per Serving: Cal 310; Prot 10 g; Carbo 50 g; Fiber 4 g;
   T Fat 9 g; Chol 8 mg; Sod 356 mg.

Dietary Exchanges: Vegetable 1; Bread/Starch 3; Meat 1/2; Fat 2

SAUCY PEPPERS ON VEGETABLE PASTA

6 cups thinly sliced onions
2 large red bell peppers, cut
   into strips
2 large yellow bell peppers,
   cut into strips
2 tablespoons sugar
2 tablespoons olive oil
2 cups chicken broth
1/4 cup cornstarch

1/4 cup water
1 tablespoon grated lemon
   rind
2 tablespoons lemon juice
1 teaspoon basil
1 teaspoon mint
Salt to taste
12 ounces uncooked tomato
   and spinach pasta

Sauté onions and peppers with sugar in olive oil in large skillet for 3 minutes; set aside. Combine broth, cornstarch dissolved in water, lemon rind, lemon juice, basil, mint and salt in saucepan. Bring to a boil, stirring constantly. Add sautéed vegetables. Heat to serving temperature, stirring frequently. Cook pasta using package directions just until tender. Ladle pepper sauce over hot pasta. Serve with Parmesan cheese. Yield: 6 servings.

Approx Per Serving: Cal 346; Prot 10 g; Carbo 65 g; Fiber 4 g;
   T Fat 6 g; Chol <1 mg; Sod 793 mg.

Dietary Exchanges: Vegetable 2 1/2; Bread/Starch 3 1/2; Meat 1/2; Fat 1

CREAMY VEGETABLE VERMICELLI

1/3 cup thinly sliced celery
1/3 cup 1/2-inch fresh green
  bean cuts
1/3 cup finely chopped carrot
1/3 cup thinly sliced red onion
1/3 cup chopped green bell
  pepper
1/2 teaspoon basil

1/8 teaspoon garlic powder
1 teaspoon olive oil
1/3 cup frozen green peas
1 teaspoon margarine
2 tablespoons flour
3/4 cup skim milk
Salt and pepper to taste
4 ounces uncooked vermicelli

Sauté celery, green beans, carrot, onion, green pepper, basil and garlic powder in olive oil in skillet until tender-crisp. Stir in peas. Melt margarine in medium saucepan. Blend in flour. Add skim milk gradually, stirring constantly. Cook until thickened, stirring constantly. Cook vermicelli using package directions; drain well. Add to cream sauce; toss until coated. Add vegetables; toss until well mixed. Serve immediately with Parmesan cheese. Yield: 2 servings.

Approx Per Serving: Cal 360; Prot 13 g; Carbo 64 g; Fiber 6 g;
  T Fat 5 g; Chol 2 mg; Sod 157 mg.

Dietary Exchanges: Milk 1/2; Vegetable 1; Bread/Starch 4; Fat 1

EXTRA-EASY VEGETABLE SOUP

1 16-ounce can whole kernel
  corn
1 16-ounce can green beans
1 16-ounce can butter beans
2 16-ounce cans whole
  tomatoes
2 cups chopped celery

2 cups sliced carrots
1 small onion, chopped
1 10-ounce can tomato soup
1 soup can milk
2 tablespoons
  Worcestershire sauce
Salt and pepper to taste

Drain corn and beans. Combine with undrained tomatoes, celery, carrots, onion, soup, milk and Worcestershire sauce in Crock•Pot. Cook on Low for several hours. Season with salt and pepper. Serve with corn muffins. Yield: 10 servings.

Approx Per Serving: Cal 221; Prot 17 g; Carbo 28 g; Fiber 5 g;
  T Fat 6 g; Chol 35 mg; Sod 700 mg.

Dietary Exchanges: Vegetable 1 1/2; Bread/Starch 1; Fat 1/2

Poultry
and Seafood

CHICKEN

BAKED HERBED CHICKEN

1   3-pound chicken, cut up
1 teaspoon rosemary
Pepper to taste
1/4 teaspoon ginger

1/2 cup unsweetened
     pineapple juice
5 green onions, minced
Paprika to taste

Rinse chicken pieces; remove and discard skin. Rub chicken with rosemary and pepper. Arrange meaty side up in 9x9-inch baking pan sprayed with nonstick cooking spray. Drizzle with mixture of ginger and pineapple juice. Sprinkle with green onions and paprika. Bake, covered, at 350 degrees for 30 minutes. Bake uncovered, for 20 minutes or until tender. Yield: 6 servings.

Approx Per Serving: Cal 236; Prot 34 g; Carbo 3 g; Fiber <1 g;
     T Fat 9 g; Chol 96 mg; Sod 80 mg.

Dietary Exchanges: Meat 4 1/2

BAKED DRUMSTICKS

10 chicken legs
2 tablespoons melted
   margarine

1/3 cup dry bread crumbs

Rinse chicken and pat dry. Brush each piece with melted margarine; coat with crumbs. Arrange in greased shallow baking pan. Bake at 375 degrees for 45 to 60 minutes or until tender. Yield: 10 servings.

Approx Per Serving: Cal 231; Prot 23 g; Carbo 2 g; Fiber 0 g;
     T Fat 14 g; Chol 78 mg; Sod 125 mg.

Dietary Exchanges: Meat 3; Fat 1

☎ Always remove skin from chicken and trim any fat to reduce calories, fat and cholesterol.

INEZ' CRISPY BAKED CHICKEN

1 3-pound chicken, cut up
5 slices bread
2/3 cup Parmesan cheese
1 tablespoon paprika
1 1/2 teaspoons seasoned salt
 substitute

1/2 teaspoon onion powder
1/2 teaspoon garlic powder
1/4 teaspoon pepper
1/2 cup skim milk

Rinse chicken pieces; remove and discard skin. Tear bread into pieces. Process in several batches in food processor until finely crumbled; this should yield approximately 1 1/2 cups. Combine crumbs, cheese, paprika, seasoned salt substitute, onion powder, garlic powder and pepper in bowl; mix well. Dip each chicken piece in milk; coat with crumbs, pressing to make thick even coating. Arrange meaty side up in 9x13-inch baking pan sprayed with nonstick cooking spray. Bake at 350 degrees for 1 hour or until chicken in brown and juices run clear when chicken is pierced with fork. Yield: 4 servings.

Approx Per Serving: Cal 509; Prot 61 g; Carbo 18 g; Fiber 1 g;
 T Fat 20 g; Chol 158 mg; Sod 605 mg.

Dietary Exchanges: Bread/Starch 1; Meat 7 1/2; Fat 1/2

CRISPY HERBED CHICKEN

6 pieces cut-up chicken
Basil, thyme, oregano,
 tarragon, paprika, salt and
 pepper to taste

2 tablespoons flour
1/3 cup warm water

Rinse chicken and pat dry. Arrange in single layer in lightly greased shallow baking dish. Combine basil, thyme, oregano, tarragon, paprika, salt, pepper and flour in small covered jar; shake to mix well. Sprinkle over chicken. Pour water down side of pan; do not pour over chicken. Bake at 375 degrees for 40 to 50 minutes or until tender, basting with pan juices occasionally. May increase measurements of herb seasonings and store unused mixture in covered jar at room temperature. Yield: 6 servings.

Approx Per Serving: Cal 177; Prot 26 g; Carbo 2 g; Fiber <1 g;
 T Fat 7 g; Chol 72 mg; Sod 60 mg.

Dietary Exchanges: Meat 3

CRUSTY BAKED CHICKEN

1 cup oats
1/3 cup Parmesan cheese
1/2 teaspoon paprika
1/2 teaspoon salt
1/8 teaspoon pepper
1   3-pound chicken, cut up
1 egg
1/4 cup milk

Process oats in blender for 1 minute. Combine with cheese, paprika, salt and pepper in bowl. Rinse chicken and discard skin; pat dry. Dip into mixture of egg and milk; coat with oat mixture. Arrange in greased baking pan. Bake at 375 degrees for 1 hour. Oat mixture may also be used to coat fish. Yield: 6 servings.

Approx Per Serving: Cal 320; Prot 40 g; Carbo 10 g; Fiber 1 g;
   T Fat 13 g; Chol 147 mg; Sod 362 mg.

Dietary Exchanges: Bread/Starch 1/2; Meat 5; Fat 1/2

CHICKEN CACCIATORE

2 cups canned tomatoes
1/2 cup tomato sauce
1/2 cup finely chopped onion
1 teaspoon chopped parsley
1/4 teaspoon garlic powder
1/4 teaspoon pepper
4 chicken breast filets

Combine tomatoes, tomato sauce, onion, parsley, garlic powder and pepper in saucepan. Simmer for 10 to 15 minutes or until onion is tender. Rinse chicken and pat dry. Arrange in baking pan. Top with sauce. Bake, covered, at 350 degrees for 1 hour or until chicken is tender. Yield: 4 servings.

Approx Per Serving: Cal 207; Prot 27 g; Carbo 9 g; Fiber 1 g;
   T Fat 7 g; Chol 72 mg; Sod 441 mg.

Dietary Exchanges: Vegetable 1 1/2; Meat 3

CHICKEN CORDON BLEU

8 chicken breast filets
8 teaspoons chopped parsley
8 thin slices mozzarella
  cheese
4 thin slices boiled ham, cut
  into halves

1 tablespoon reduced-calorie
  mayonnaise
1 tablespoon warm water
1/4 cup seasoned bread
  crumbs

Rinse chicken and pat dry. Pound to flatten; sprinkle with parsley. Layer 1 slice of cheese and ham on each filet; roll tightly to enclose filling. Dip each roll in mixture of mayonnaise and water; coat with bread crumbs. Place seam side down on greased baking sheet. Bake at 425 degrees for 15 to 20 minutes or until brown. Serve with Skim Milk White Sauce (page 125) if desired. Yield: 8 servings.

Approx Per Serving: Cal 292; Prot 34 g; Carbo 4 g; Fiber <1 g;
    T Fat 15 g; Chol 103 mg; Sod 377 mg.

Dietary Exchanges: Meat 4 1/2; Fat 1

MUSHROOM DIJON CHICKEN

2 pounds chicken breast filets
16 ounces mushrooms, sliced

1 1/2 cups white wine
1   8-ounce jar Dijon mustard

Rinse chicken and pat dry. Layer mushrooms and chicken in 9x13-inch baking dish. Pour mixture of wine and mustard over chicken. Marinate for 15 minutes. Bake at 350 degrees for 35 minutes. Serve with wild rice. Yield: 8 servings.

Approx Per Serving: Cal 240; Prot 27 g; Carbo 4 g; Fiber 1 g;
    T Fat 7 g; Chol 72 mg; Sod 457 mg.
    Nutritional information includes entire amount of marinade.

Dietary Exchanges: Vegetable 1/2; Meat 3

FRUITED CHICKEN BREASTS

6 chicken breast filets
1 tablespoon margarine
1/4 teaspoon cardamom
Salt and pepper to taste
3 cups thinly sliced unpeeled
  apples
1/3 cup apple cider
1/4 cup sugar

1 tablespoon lemon juice
1 1/2 teaspoons grated lemon
  rind
1 teaspoon Worcestershire
  sauce
1 teaspoon cream-style
  horseradish

Rinse chicken and pat dry. Arrange in shallow baking dish. Dot with margarine; sprinkle with cardamom, salt and pepper. Bake at 350 degrees for 30 minutes or until tender. Combine apples, cider, sugar, lemon juice, lemon rind, Worcestershire sauce and horseradish in medium saucepan. Simmer over medium-low heat until apples are tender. Pour over chicken. Bake just until heated through. Yield: 6 servings.

Approx Per Serving: Cal 253; Prot 26 g; Carbo 17 g; Fiber 1 g;
    T Fat 9 g; Chol 72 mg; Sod 99 mg.

Dietary Exchanges: Fruit 1/2; Meat 3; Fat 1/2

CHICKEN BREASTS VERONIQUE

8 chicken breast filets
1 cup cracker crumbs
1/2 teaspoon tarragon
Salt and pepper to taste
3 tablespoons margarine
1/4 cup chopped onion

1/2 cup chicken broth
1/2 cup dry white wine
2 cups sliced fresh
  mushrooms
2 tablespoons margarine
2 cups green grapes

Rinse chicken and pat dry. Combine cracker crumbs, tarragon, salt and pepper in bowl. Coat chicken with crumb mixture. Brown in 3 tablespoons margarine in skillet. Remove to shallow baking dish. Sauté onion in drippings in skillet; drain. Add broth and wine, stirring to deglaze skillet. Bring to a boil. Pour over chicken. Bake at 375 degrees for 30 minutes. Sauté mushrooms in 2 tablespoons margarine in skillet. Spoon mushrooms and grapes around chicken. Bake for 10 minutes longer. Yield: 8 servings.

Approx Per Serving: Cal 308; Prot 27 g; Carbo 12 g; Fiber 1 g;
    T Fat 15 g; Chol 75 mg; Sod 330 mg.

Dietary Exchanges: Vegetable 1/2; Fruit 1/2; Bread/Starch 1/2; Meat 3 1/2; Fat 2

LEMON-BAKED CHICKEN BREASTS

4 chicken breasts, skinned
1/2 cup flour
Salt and pepper to taste
1 egg
1/2 cup water

1 stack Waverly crackers,
   crushed
Juice of 1 lemon
1/4 cup melted margarine

Rinse chicken and pat dry. Shake with mixture of flour, salt and pepper in bag. Beat egg with water in bowl. Dip chicken in egg; coat with cracker crumbs. Arrange meaty side up in 9x13-inch baking dish. Bake at 400 degrees for 10 minutes. Brush with mixture of lemon juice and margarine. Bake until chicken is tender, basting occasionally with lemon mixture. Serve hot or cold. Yield: 4 servings.

Approx Per Serving: Cal 384; Prot 29 g; Carbo 17 g; Fiber <1 g;
   T Fat 21 g; Chol 141 mg; Sod 274 mg.

Dietary Exchanges: Bread/Starch 1; Meat 3 1/2; Fat 2 1/2

LAGO LEMON CHICKEN

1 cup whole wheat bread
   crumbs
1 1/2 teaspoons minced parsley
1 1/2 teaspoons grated lemon
   rind
1 teaspoon basil

1/2 teaspoon salt
1/2 teaspoon pepper
6 chicken breasts, skinned
3 tablespoons buttermilk
1 3/4 teaspoons lemon juice

Mix bread crumbs, parsley, lemon rind, basil, salt and pepper in plastic bag. Rinse chicken and pat dry. Brush with mixture of buttermilk and lemon juice. Place on rack sprayed with nonstick cooking spray in baking pan. Sprinkle with bread crumb mixture. Bake at 350 degrees for 40 minutes or until tender. Garnish with additional parsley. Yield: 6 servings.

Approx Per Serving: Cal 194; Prot 27 g; Carbo 5 g; Fiber 1 g;
   T Fat 7 g; Chol 72 mg; Sod 290 mg.

Dietary Exchanges: Bread/Starch 1/2; Meat 3

☎ Reduce cholesterol in **Lemon-Baked Chicken Breasts** by substituting 2 egg whites for whole egg.

CHICKEN À L'ORANGE

2 chicken breasts
1½ cups tomato juice
¼ cup chopped onion
½ cup chopped green bell
  pepper
½ cup chopped celery
¼ cup thawed frozen orange
  juice concentrate

1 teaspoon mustard
2 tablespoons soy sauce
2 tablespoons
  Worcestershire sauce
½ teaspoon Tabasco sauce
Garlic powder to taste

Rinse chicken and pat dry. Arrange in baking dish. Combine tomato juice, onion, green pepper, celery, orange juice concentrate, mustard, soy sauce, Worcestershire sauce, Tabasco sauce and garlic powder in saucepan. Cook until thickened, stirring constantly. Spoon over chicken. Bake at 350 degrees for 1½ hours. Yield: 2 servings.

Approx Per Serving: Cal 285; Prot 30 g; Carbo 26 g; Fiber 3 g;
    T Fat 7 g; Chol 72 mg; Sod 1964 mg.

Dietary Exchanges: Vegetable 2; Fruit 1; Meat 3½

CHICKEN POTPIE

1 cup reduced-sodium
  chicken broth
¼ cup chopped onion
1 tablespoon cornstarch
½ cup cold skim milk
⅛ teaspoon pepper
2 tablespoons chopped
  parsley
1 cup chopped cooked
  chicken

½ cup chopped cooked
  potato
½ cup chopped cooked carrot
1 5-ounce can corn, drained
1 cup crushed bran flakes
1 tablespoon oil
½ teaspoon each marjoram,
  tarragon and oregano

Combine chicken broth and onion in saucepan. Stir in mixture of cornstarch and milk gradually. Cook over medium heat until thickened, stirring constantly. Stir in pepper and parsley. Layer chicken, potato, carrot and corn in 1-quart baking dish. Spoon sauce over layers. Combine bran flake crumbs, oil, marjoram, tarragon and oregano in small bowl; mix well. Sprinkle over layers. Bake at 350 degrees for 30 minutes or until bubbly. Yield: 4 servings.

Approx Per Serving: Cal 304; Prot 22 g; Carbo 40 g; Fiber 6 g;
    T Fat 9 g; Chol 42 mg; Sod 431 mg.

Dietary Exchanges: Vegetable ½; Bread/Starch 2½; Meat 2; Fat 1

CHICKEN WITH WILD RICE

8 chicken breasts
1 large green bell pepper, chopped
4 stalks celery, chopped

1½ cups chicken broth
⅔ cup uncooked wild rice
2 tablespoons soy sauce
2 green onions, chopped

Rinse chicken and pat dry; remove skin. Combine green pepper, celery, broth and rice in bowl; mix well. Spoon into large baking dish. Brush chicken with soy sauce. Arrange over rice mixture. Bake, covered, at 350 degrees for 1½ hours. Sprinkle with green onions. Yield: 4 servings.

Approx Per Serving: Cal 460; Prot 58 g; Carbo 24 g; Fiber 1 g; T Fat 14 g; Chol 144 mg; Sod 963 mg.

Dietary Exchanges: Vegetable ½; Bread/Starch 1½; Meat 6½

BRAISED CHICKEN BREASTS

½ cup plain nonfat yogurt
2 tablespoons Dijon mustard

4 chicken breast filets
Mrs. Dash seasoning to taste

Combine yogurt and mustard in small bowl; mix well. Rinse chicken and pat dry; sprinkle with Mrs. Dash seasoning. Heat skillet sprayed with nonstick cooking spray over low heat until hot but not smoking. Add chicken; increase heat to medium. Cook chicken for 7 to 10 minutes on each side or until cooked through. Serve hot with mustard sauce. Store unused mustard sauce, covered, in refrigerator. Yield: 4 servings.

Approx Per Serving: Cal 191; Prot 27 g; Carbo 2 g; Fiber <1 g; T Fat 7 g; Chol 73 mg; Sod 179 mg.

Dietary Exchanges: Milk ½; Meat 3

☎ Make a **Tangy Topper** of 1 cup low-fat cottage cheese, ¼ cup plain nonfat yogurt and ½ teaspoon lemon juice blended until smooth. Use as a topper or as an alternative to sour cream.

BROCCOLI CHICKEN

2 large chicken breast filets
Salt and pepper to taste
1/4 cup chopped onion
2 tablespoons margarine
1 teaspoon lemon juice

1 10-ounce package frozen
    chopped broccoli, thawed
1/4 teaspoon thyme
3 medium tomatoes, cut into
    wedges

Rinse chicken and pat dry; cut into bite-sized pieces. Sprinkle with salt and pepper. Sauté chicken and onion in margarine in skillet. Add lemon juice, broccoli, thyme, salt and pepper. Simmer, covered, for 6 minutes. Add tomatoes. Simmer, covered, for 4 minutes longer. Yield: 4 servings.

Approx Per Serving: Cal 259; Prot 29 g; Carbo 7 g; Fiber 5 g;
    T Fat 13 g; Chol 72 mg; Sod 151 mg.

Dietary Exchanges: Vegetable 2; Meat 3; Fat 1 1/2

CHICKEN CURRY

1 3 1/2-pound chicken
2 small onions, chopped
1 clove of garlic, minced
1 stalk celery, chopped
1/4 cup margarine
1 apple, peeled, chopped

1/4 cup flour
6 tablespoons curry powder
1/2 teaspoon dry mustard
Salt to taste
1 bay leaf
1 cup milk

Rinse chicken. Cook in water to cover in saucepan until tender. Drain, reserving 3 cups chicken broth. Chop chicken. Sauté onions, garlic and celery in margarine in skillet. Add apple. Stir in flour, curry powder, dry mustard and salt. Cook over medium-low heat for 2 minutes, stirring constantly. Add bay leaf. Stir in reserved broth gradually. Cook until thickened, stirring constantly. Cook, covered, over low heat for 30 minutes. Add chicken and milk. Simmer for several minutes or until heated through. Remove bay leaf. Serve over hot cooked rice. Serve with small bowls of toppings such as raisins, peanuts, chopped cantaloupe, chopped honeydew, chopped tomatoes, chopped hard-boiled eggs, shredded Cheddar cheese, pineapple chunks and orange sections. Yield: 6 servings.

Approx Per Serving: Cal 417; Prot 41 g; Carbo 16 g; Fiber 1 g;
    T Fat 20 g; Chol 118 mg; Sod 211 mg.
    Nutritional information does not include toppings.

Dietary Exchanges: Vegetable 1/2; Fruit 1/2; Bread/Starch 1/2; Meat 5; Fat 2

CHICKEN DIJON

4 chicken breast filets
3 tablespoons margarine
2 tablespoons flour

1 cup chicken broth
1/2 cup half and half
2 tablespoons Dijon mustard

Rinse chicken and pat dry. Sauté in margarine in skillet for 20 minutes. Remove to warm platter. Stir flour into drippings in skillet. Add broth and half and half. Simmer until thickened, stirring constantly. Stir in mustard. Add chicken. Cook, covered, for 10 minutes. Yield: 4 servings.

Approx Per Serving: Cal 314; Prot 28 g; Carbo 5 g; Fiber <1 g;
     T Fat 19 g; Chol 83 mg; Sod 463 mg.

Dietary Exchanges: Bread/Starch 1/2; Meat 3 1/2; Fat 2 1/2

CHICKEN WITH GRAPES

4 chicken breast filets
1/2 cup apple juice
**1 teaspoon instant chicken
   bouillon**

1 teaspoon cornstarch
1/4 teaspoon dried mint
**1 cup seedless red and green
   grape halves**

Rinse chicken and pat dry. Preheat large skillet sprayed with nonstick cooking spray over medium heat. Add chicken. Cook for 8 to 10 minutes or until cooked through, turning to brown evenly. Remove to warm plate. Combine apple juice, bouillon, cornstarch and mint in saucepan. Cook until thickened, stirring constantly. Cook for 2 minutes longer. Stir in grape halves. Cook until heated through. Serve over chicken. Yield: 4 servings.

Approx Per Serving: Cal 201; Prot 26 g; Carbo 8 g; Fiber <1 g;
     T Fat 7 g; Chol 72 mg; Sod 349 mg.

Dietary Exchanges: Fruit 1/2; Meat 3

☎ Substitute plain nonfat yogurt or evaporated skim milk for half and half or cream to reduce fat, cholesterol and calories in creamy sauces. For lighter clear sauces use chicken broth.

CHICKEN ITALIANO

4 chicken breasts
1 14-ounce can tomatoes
1/2 teaspoon basil
1/2 teaspoon tarragon
1/4 teaspoon pepper
1 clove of garlic, chopped
2 teaspoons oil
2 tablespoons chopped
parsley
1/2 cup shredded mozzarella
cheese

Rinse chicken and pat dry. Combine tomatoes, basil, tarragon and pepper in blender container; process until smooth. Sauté garlic in oil in skillet for 1 minute. Add chicken rib side up. Pour tomato mixture over top. Bring to a boil; reduce heat. Simmer for 15 minutes or until chicken is tender. Arrange chicken in baking dish. Stir parsley into sauce in skillet. Pour over chicken. Sprinkle with cheese. Broil for 1 minute or until cheese melts. Yield: 4 servings.

Approx Per Serving: Cal 249; Prot 29 g; Carbo 5 g; Fiber <1 g;
T Fat 12 g; Chol 83 mg; Sod 276 mg.

Dietary Exchanges: Vegetable 1; Meat 3 1/2; Fat 1

ORANGE-GLAZED CHICKEN AND VEGETABLES

4 chicken breast filets
2 tablespoons flour
1/2 teaspoon paprika
Pepper to taste
1 tablespoon oil
1/4 cup orange juice
1/4 cup orange marmalade
1 16-ounce can whole baby
carrots, drained
1 10-ounce package frozen
peas and onions
1 tablespoon orange
marmalade

Rinse chicken and pat dry. Coat with mixture of flour, paprika and pepper. Brown for 3 minutes on each side in oil in skillet. Combine orange juice and 1/4 cup marmalade in bowl. Pour over chicken. Simmer for 6 minutes. Remove chicken to warm platter. Add carrots, peas and onions to drippings in skillet. Arrange chicken on vegetables. Brush with remaining 1 tablespoon marmalade. Simmer, covered, over medium heat for 5 minutes longer. Yield: 4 servings.

Approx Per Serving: Cal 345; Prot 28 g; Carbo 34 g; Fiber <1 g;
T Fat 10 g; Chol 72 mg; Sod 108 mg.

Dietary Exchanges: Vegetable 1/2; Bread/Starch 1; Meat 3; Fat 1/2

MANDARIN CHICKEN WITH BROCCOLI

8 chicken breast filets
1/4 cup unbleached flour
1 tablespoon paprika
Salt and pepper to taste
1/4 cup minced onion
3 tablespoons margarine

1 cup chicken broth
1 cup skim milk
1 1/2 pounds broccoli
1   8-ounce can mandarin
    oranges, drained

Rinse chicken and pat dry. Shake 1 piece at a time in mixture of flour, paprika, salt and pepper in bag. Sauté onion in margarine in skillet over medium-high heat. Add chicken. Sauté for 5 minutes on each side. Remove chicken. Add broth. Bring to a boil over medium heat. Cook for 5 minutes, stirring frequently. Add milk. Simmer for 5 minutes, stirring frequently. Add chicken; baste with sauce. Simmer over low heat for 10 minutes, basting frequently. Remove flowerets from broccoli; slice stems. Steam broccoli in a small amount of water in saucepan until tender. Arrange chicken in center of serving plate; arrange broccoli around chicken. Spoon sauce over chicken and broccoli. Top with orange sections. Yield: 8 servings.

Approx Per Serving: Cal 280; Prot 30 g; Carbo 15 g; Fiber 4 g;
     T Fat 12 g; Chol 73 mg; Sod 248 mg.

Dietary Exchanges: Vegetable 1; Fruit 1/2; Meat 3 1/2; Fat 1

CHICKEN PICCATA

4 chicken breast filets
1/4 teaspoon garlic powder
1/4 teaspoon onion powder
Salt and pepper to taste
1/4 cup self-rising flour
3 tablespoons margarine

1 clove of garlic, minced
1 cup sliced fresh mushrooms
1/4 cup white wine
2 tablespoons lemon juice
2 tablespoons chopped
    parsley

Rinse chicken and pat dry. Pound 1/2 inch thick between plastic wrap. Sprinkle with garlic powder, onion powder, salt and pepper; coat with flour. Brown lightly in margarine in skillet over medium heat. Remove to warm platter. Add garlic and mushrooms to drippings in skillet. Sauté until tender. Add chicken, wine and lemon juice. Simmer for 7 to 10 minutes or until sauce is thickened to desired consistency, stirring occasionally. Top with parsley. Yield: 4 servings.

Approx Per Serving: Cal 289; Prot 27 g; Carbo 8 g; Fiber <1 g;
     T Fat 15 g; Chol 72 mg; Sod 254 mg.

Dietary Exchanges: Bread/Starch 1/2; Meat 3; Fat 2

CHICKEN SCALLOPINI

4 chicken breast filets
2 tablespoons Parmesan
  cheese

2 tablespoons seasoned
  bread crumbs
1/2 cup dry Sherry

Rinse chicken. Coat with mixture of cheese and bread crumbs. Cook in nonstick skillet sprayed with nonstick cooking spray for 8 minutes or until golden, turning once. Remove to serving plate. Add Sherry to skillet, stirring to deglaze. Cook over high heat until wine is reduced by half. Pour over chicken. Garnish with parsley and additional cheese. Yield: 4 servings.

Approx Per Serving: Cal 234; Prot 27 g; Carbo 5 g; Fiber 0 g;
    T Fat 8 g; Chol 75 mg; Sod 142 mg.

Dietary Exchanges: Meat 3 1/2

CHICKEN STEW

2/3 cup chopped onion
1/2 cup chopped green bell
  pepper
1/2 cup sliced celery
1   15-ounce can no-salt-
  added tomatoes, chopped
1   10-ounce can reduced-
  sodium tomato soup

2/3 cup dry white wine
Garlic powder and red pepper
  to taste
2   5-ounce cans water-pack
  chunk white chicken
1/2 cup uncooked instant rice

Sauté onion, green pepper and celery in saucepan sprayed with nonstick cooking spray. Add tomatoes, soup, wine, garlic powder and red pepper. Bring to a boil; reduce heat. Simmer for 20 minutes. Stir in chicken and rice; remove from heat. Let stand, covered, for 5 minutes. Fluff with fork before serving. Yield: 5 servings.

Approx Per Serving: Cal 256; Prot 16 g; Carbo 30 g; Fiber 2 g;
    T Fat 6 g; Chol 31 mg; Sod 601 mg.

Dietary Exchanges: Vegetable 1; Starch/Bread 1 1/2; Meat 1 1/2

1963

MICROWAVE STUFFED CHICKEN ROLLS

4 chicken breast filets
1/3 cup ricotta cheese
2 tablespoons Parmesan
  cheese
1 tablespoon sliced green
  onion
1/4 teaspoon oregano

1/8 teaspoon thyme
Salt and pepper to taste
1 15-ounce jar thick
  spaghetti sauce
1 1/2 cups shredded
  mozzarella cheese

Rinse chicken and pat dry. Pound 1/4 inch thick between plastic wrap. Combine ricotta cheese, Parmesan cheese, green onion, oregano, thyme, salt and pepper in bowl; mix well. Spoon onto chicken filets. Fold in sides and roll filets to enclose filling; secure with wooden picks. Place seam side down in glass 9x9-inch baking dish. Pour spaghetti sauce over top. Microwave, loosely covered with waxed paper, on High for 11 to 15 minutes or just until chicken is tender, turning dish twice. Remove picks; sprinkle with mozzarella cheese. Microwave on Medium for 2 to 4 minutes or until cheese melts. Serve with pasta. Yield: 4 servings.

Approx Per Serving: Cal 456; Prot 39 g; Carbo 19 g; Fiber <1 g;
    T Fat 25 g; Chol 118 mg; Sod 824 mg.

Dietary Exchanges: Vegetable 1 1/2; Meat 5 1/2; Fat 2 1/2

MICROWAVE CHICKEN ROLL-UPS

4 chicken breast filets
1/4 teaspoon garlic powder
2 slices mozzarella cheese,
  cut into halves

12 asparagus spears
1/4 cup Parmesan cheese
1/4 teaspoon paprika

Rinse chicken; pound to flatten. Sprinkle with garlic powder. Top each filet with 1/2 slice mozzarella cheese and 3 asparagus spears. Roll to enclose filling; secure with wooden picks. Place seam down in glass dish. Microwave, loosely covered, on High for 3 minutes. Sprinkle with Parmesan cheese and paprika. Let stand for 5 minutes. Yield: 4 servings.

Approx Per Serving: Cal 262; Prot 33 g; Carbo 5 g; Fiber 1 g;
    T Fat 12 g; Chol 88 mg; Sod 233 mg.

Dietary Exchanges: Vegetable 1; Meat 4; Fat 1/2

MICROWAVE ORANGE CHICKEN WITH LEMON PEPPER

4 chicken breast filets
1 tablespoon Parmesan
  cheese
1 tablespoon chopped parsley
2 teaspoons grated orange
  rind

1/4 cup orange juice
1 tablespoon dry white wine
1 teaspoon lemon juice
Sections of 4 medium
  oranges
2 teaspoons lemon pepper

Rinse chicken and pat dry. Arrange in 9-inch glass plate with meaty portions toward outer edge. Sprinkle with cheese, parsley and orange rind; drizzle with orange juice, wine and lemon juice. Microwave, tightly covered, on High for 4 minutes. Turn chicken. Place oranges in center of plate. Microwave, tightly covered, for 2 to 6 minutes or until chicken is tender. Baste with pan juices. Sprinkle with lemon pepper. Yield: 4 servings.

Approx Per Serving: Cal 246; Prot 27 g; Carbo 17 g; Fiber 3 g;
    T Fat 7 g; Chol 73 mg; Sod 92 mg.

Dietary Exchanges: Fruit 1 1/2; Meat 3 1/2

MICROWAVE CALIFORNIA CHICKEN

4 chicken breast filets
2 teaspoons lemon juice
1 teaspoon onion flakes
Basil and pepper to taste

2/3 cup shredded sharp
  Cheddar cheese
1/2 avocado, thinly sliced
4 thin tomato slices

Rinse chicken and pat dry. Arrange in glass baking dish. Sprinkle with lemon juice, onion flakes, basil and pepper. Microwave, covered with waxed paper, on High for 7 1/2 minutes or until chicken is tender, turning dish twice. Sprinkle with half the cheese. Arrange avocado and tomato on top. Microwave, covered, for 2 1/2 minutes. Sprinkle with remaining cheese. Let stand, covered, for 5 minutes. Yield: 4 servings.

Approx Per Serving: Cal 287; Prot 30 g; Carbo 3 g; Fiber 1 g;
    T Fat 17 g; Chol 92 mg; Sod 181 mg.

Dietary Exchanges: Vegetable 1/2; Meat 4; Fat 2

STIR-FRY ALMOND CHICKEN WITH RICE

6 chicken breast filets
Garlic salt to taste
1 10-ounce package frozen
   oriental vegetables
1 cup thinly sliced celery
1/3 cup chicken broth
1 tablespoon cornstarch
2 tablespoons reduced-
   sodium soy sauce

1 teaspoon sugar
1/2 cup chicken broth
1/2 cup slivered almonds
1 cup drained fresh pineapple
   chunks
3 cups hot cooked rice
1/3 cup thinly sliced green
   onions

Rinse chicken and pat dry; cut into thin strips. Sprinkle with garlic salt. Preheat nonstick skillet sprayed with nonstick cooking spray. Add chicken. Stir-fry until light brown on all sides. Add oriental vegetables, celery and 1/3 cup broth. Cook, covered, for 3 mintues. Blend conrstarch, soy sauce, sugar and 1/2 cup broth in small bowl. Stir into chicken mixture. Cook until thickened, stirring constantly. Stir in half the almonds and pineapple. Cook for several seconds until heated through. Spoon over rice. Sprinkle remaining almonds and green onions over top. Yield: 6 servings.

Approx Per Serving: Cal 377; Prot 32 g; Carbo 35 g; Fiber 3 g;
    T Fat 12 g; Chol 72 mg; Sod 462 mg.

Dietary Exchanges: Vegetable 1; Fruit 1/2; Bread/Starch 1 1/2; Meat 3 1/2; Fat 1

SAUTÉED CHICKEN WITH APPLE

1 pound chicken breast filets
1 tablespoon safflower oil
1 cup diagonally sliced celery
1 medium green bell pepper,
   sliced lengthwise
1 medium onion, sliced
1 tart apple, sliced

1/2 cup apple juice
1 tablespoon white wine
   vinegar
1 tablespoon cornstarch
1 teaspoon reduced-sodium
   soy sauce

Rinse chicken and pat dry; slice into strips. Sauté in oil in nonstick skillet over medium heat. Remove to warm plate. Add celery, green pepper and onion. Sauté until tender-crisp. Add chicken and apple. Sauté for 1 minute. Combine remaining ingredients in bowl. Add to skillet. Cook until thickened, stirring constantly. Yield: 4 servings.

Approx Per Serving: Cal 263; Prot 26 g; Carbo 16 g; Fiber 2 g;
    T Fat 10 g; Chol 72 mg; Sod 153 mg.

Dietary Exchanges: Vegetable 1; Fruit 1/2; Meat 3; Fat 1/2

STIR-FRY SZECHUAN CHICKEN

4 chicken breast filets
1 egg, slightly beaten
1/4 cup flour
2 tablespoons oil
2 tablespoons steak sauce
1/4 cup Worcestershire sauce
2 tablespoons sugar
2 tablespoons tomato sauce

2 tablespoons vinegar
Salt to taste
1 dried chili pepper, crushed
2 tablespoons chopped
  gingerroot
2 tablespoons chopped green
  onions

Rinse chicken and pat dry; slice into thin strips. Dip in egg; coat with flour. Stir-fry in oil in wok until golden brown. Remove with slotted spoon; drain wok. Combine steak sauce, Worcestershire sauce, sugar, tomato sauce, vinegar and salt in small bowl; mix well. Add to wok. Bring to a boil. Stir in chili pepper, gingerroot and green onions. Simmer for several seconds. Add chicken, stirring gently to coat well. Cook until heated through. Yield: 4 servings.

Approx Per Serving: Cal 332; Prot 28 g; Carbo 20 g; Fiber <1 g;
     T Fat 15 g; Chol 141 mg; Sod 296 mg.

Dietary Exchanges: Vegetable 1; Bread/Starch 1/2; Meat 3 1/2; Fat 1 1/2

PINEAPPLE CHICKEN (PO LO CHI)

1 pound chicken breast filets
1 tablespoon cornstarch
1 teaspoon salt
2 teaspoons cold water
1 tablespoon soy sauce
1 1/2 cups lengthwise sliced
  onions

3 tablespoons oil
1 cup diagonally sliced celery
10 water chestnuts, sliced
4 slices pineapple, cut into
  wedges
1/4 cup pineapple juice

Rinse chicken and pat dry; cut into 1-inch pieces. Combine cornstarch, salt, water and soy sauce in bowl. Add chicken, coating well. Stir-fry onions in 1 tablespoon oil in wok for 2 minutes. Remove to bowl. Add celery, water chestnuts and 1 tablespoon oil. Stir-fry for 2 minutes. Remove to bowl. Add chicken and 1 tablespoon oil. Stir-fry until brown. Add stir-fried vegetables, pineapple and pineapple juice. Simmer until heated through. Serve over rice. Yield: 6 servings.

Approx Per Serving: Cal 219; Prot 18 g; Carbo 11 g; Fiber 1 g;
     T Fat 11 g; Chol 48 mg; Sod 558 mg.

Dietary Exchanges: Vegetable 1; Meat 2; Fat 1 1/2

TURKEY

ROAST TURKEY

1 14-pound turkey
Salt and pepper to taste

³/₄ cup melted margarine
¹/₂ cup Courvoisier

Rinse turkey inside and out; pat dry. Sprinkle cavity with salt and pepper. Brush outside with ¹/₄ cup melted margarine. Place on side on rack in roasting pan. Roast at 425 degrees for 15 minutes. Heat remaining ¹/₂ cup margarine with Courvoisier in small saucepan over low heat. Brush over turkey; turn to other side. Roast for 15 minutes. Baste turkey with sauce; turn breast side up. Reduce oven temperature to 325 degrees. Roast turkey for 3 to 3¹/₂ hours or until tender, basting every 20 minutes. Place on serving platter. Let stand for 20 to 30 minutes before carving. May thicken pan drippings for gravy. Yield: 10 servings.

Approx Per Serving: Cal 689; Prot 93 g; Carbo <1 g; Fiber 0 g;
   T Fat 29 g; Chol 243 mg; Sod 383 mg.

Dietary Exchanges: Meat 11; Fat 3

SMOKED TURKEY

2 quarts apple juice
2 cups dry white wine
1 small red onion, chopped
3 large cloves of garlic,
   chopped
10 whole peppercorns

¹/₄ cup sugar
1 tablespoon rosemary
1 tablespoon thyme
1 small bay leaf
Noniodized salt to taste
1 12-pound turkey

Combine apple juice, wine, onion, garlic, peppercorns, sugar, rosemary, thyme, bay leaf and salt in large stockpot. Bring to a boil, stirring to dissolve sugar. Cool completely. Combine with turkey in large plastic bag; seal tightly. Marinate in refrigerator for 8 hours or longer. Drain and rinse turkey; pat dry inside and out. Place in smoker. Smoke for 2¹/₂ to 3 hours; pat dry inside. Place in roasting pan. Roast using directions on turkey wrapper, decreasing roasting time by 10% for each hour of smoking time. Yield: 10 servings.

Approx Per Serving: Cal 611; Prot 80 g; Carbo 29 g; Fiber <1 g;
   T Fat 14 g; Chol 208 mg; Sod 228 mg.
   Nutritional information includes entire amount of marinade.

Dietary Exchanges: Fruit 1¹/₂; Meat 9¹/₂

TURKEY AND BEAN SKILLET

1 pound ground turkey
1 tablespoon oil
1 small onion, chopped
2 14-ounce cans pork and
   beans

1 4-ounce can tomato sauce
Garlic powder to taste
1 teaspoon salt 'n spices
   seasoning

Brown turkey in oil in skillet, stirring until crumbly; drain. Add onion, pork and beans, tomato sauce and seasonings; mix well. Simmer for 15 minutes. Yield: 6 servings.

Approx Per Serving: Cal 259; Prot 24 g; Carbo 28 g; Fiber 8 g;
    T Fat 7 g; Chol 52 mg; Sod 712 mg.

Dietary Exchanges: Vegetable 1/2; Bread/Starch 1 1/2; Meat 2 1/2; Fat 1

TURKEY CHILI

1 pound ground turkey
1 16-ounce can brown beans
1 1/4 cups tomato sauce
1/2 cup chopped onion
1/4 cup chopped celery
1 clove of garlic, minced
1 tablespoon chili powder

1/4 teaspoon cumin
2 cups drained canned
   tomatoes
1/4 cup chopped green bell
   pepper
1/2 cup thinly sliced carrot
1/8 teaspoon pepper

Brown ground turkey in large saucepan, stirring until crumbly. Add beans, tomato sauce, onion, celery, garlic, chili powder, cumin, tomatoes, green pepper, carrot and pepper; mix well. Simmer for 2 hours, stirring frequently. Yield: 6 servings.

Approx Per Serving: Cal 210; Prot 23 g; Carbo 23 g; Fiber 5 g;
    T Fat 4 g; Chol 43 mg; Sod 747 mg.

Dietary Exchanges: Vegetable 1 1/2; Bread/Starch 1; Meat 2

☎ Remove most of the fat from ground turkey or ground beef by microwaving in plastic colander placed in glass bowl to catch drippings.

TURKEY GOULASH

1 pound ground turkey
1 small onion, finely chopped
1/4 green bell pepper, chopped
Chopped garlic to taste
1 tablespoon oil
1 14-ounce can stewed
  tomatoes
1 4-ounce can tomato paste
1 14-ounce can water
1/2 teaspoon Italian seasoning
1 teaspoon salt 'n spices
  seasoning
1 1/2 cups uncooked elbow
  macaroni

Brown ground turkey with onion, green pepper and garlic in oil in skillet, stirring until ground turkey is crumbly; drain. Add tomatoes, tomato paste, water, and seasonings. Bring to a boil. Add macaroni; reduce heat. Simmer, covered, for 20 minutes or until macaroni is tender. Yield: 6 servings.

Approx Per Serving: Cal 259; Prot 22 g; Carbo 30 g; Fiber 2 g;
    T Fat 6 g; Chol 43 mg; Sod 161 mg.

Dietary Exchanges: Vegetable 1 1/2; Bread/Starch 1 1/2; Meat 2; Fat 1/2

TURKEY LOAF

1 pound ground turkey
1 egg
1 stalk celery, finely chopped
1 small onion, finely chopped
1 tablespoon (or more) sage
1 cup (or less) bread crumbs
1 teaspoon salt 'n spices
  seasoning
1 tablespoon bread crumbs
1/4 cup melted margarine

Combine ground turkey, egg, celery, onion, sage, 1 cup bread crumbs and seasoning in bowl; mix well. Pack into baking pan. Sprinkle with 1 tablespoon bread crumbs; drizzle with margarine. Bake at 375 degrees for 30 to 45 minutes or until done to taste. May add chopped green pepper or top tomato sauce instead of margarine. Yield: 6 servings.

Approx Per Serving: Cal 255; Prot 20 g; Carbo 15 g; Fiber <1 g;
    T Fat 12 g; Chol 89 mg; Sod 277 mg.

Dietary Exchanges: Vegetable 1/2; Bread/Starch 1; Meat 2; Fat 2

TURKEY PIZZAS

8 ounces ground turkey
1 small onion, chopped
1/4 green bell pepper, chopped
1 tablespoon oil
1 4-ounce can sliced
   mushrooms, drained

1 16-ounce can pizza sauce
Oregano and garlic powder to
   taste
6 English muffins, split
2 cups shredded mozzarella
   cheese

Brown ground turkey with onion and green pepper in oil in skillet, stirring until ground turkey is crumbly; drain. Add mushrooms, pizza sauce, oregano and garlic powder; mix well. Arrange muffins cut side up on baking sheet. Spread turkey mixture over muffins; sprinkle with cheese. Bake at 400 degrees for 5 minutes or until cheese melts. May add 1 dissolved beef bouillon cube to turkey mixture for a beefy flavor. Yield: 6 servings.

Approx Per Serving: Cal 404; Prot 22 g; Carbo 41 g; Fiber <1 g;
   T Fat 17 g; Chol 51 mg; Sod 897 mg.

Dietary Exchanges: Vegetable 2 1/2; Bread/Starch 2; Meat 2 1/2; Fat 2

TURKEY POLYNESIAN

1 tablespoon cornstarch
2 teaspoons water
1 teaspoon reduced-sodium
   soy sauce
Salt to taste
1 1/2 pounds turkey breast
   filets
1 cup sliced onion

1 1/2 teaspoons oil
1 cup diagonally sliced celery
1 8-ounce can sliced water
   chestnuts, drained
1 tablespoon oil
1 cup drained juice-pack
   pineapple chunks
1/4 cup pineapple juice

Blend cornstarch, water, soy sauce and salt in bowl. Rinse turkey and pat dry; cut into bite-sized pieces. Add to cornstarch mixture, stirring to coat well. Sauté onion in 1 1/2 teaspoons oil in skillet over medium heat. Add celery and water chestnuts. Cook for 2 minutes. Remove vegetables with slotted spoon. Add remaining 1 tablespoon oil and turkey to skillet. Sauté until brown. Add vegetables, pineapple and pineapple juice. Simmer for 10 minutes. Serve with hot rice. Yield: 6 servings.

Approx Per Serving: Cal 200; Prot 27 g; Carbo 13 g; Fiber 1 g;
   T Fat 4 g; Chol 71 mg; Sod 109 mg.

Dietary Exchanges: Vegetable 1 1/2; Fruit 1/2; Meat 2 1/2; Fat 1/2

TURKEY SPAGHETTI SAUCE

8 ounces ground turkey
1 small onion, chopped
1/4 green bell pepper, chopped
1 teaspoon oil
1 beef bouillon cube
1 16-ounce jar spaghetti
sauce

1 4-ounce can sliced
mushrooms, drained
1/2 teaspoon garlic salt
1/2 teaspoon salt 'n spices
seasoning

Brown turkey with onion and green pepper in oil in skillet, stirring until ground turkey is crumbly; drain. Dissolve bouillon cube in a small amount of water. Add bouillon, spaghetti sauce, mushrooms and seasonings to turkey; mix well. Simmer for 20 minutes. Serve over spaghetti. Yield: 4 servings.

Approx Per Serving: Cal 227; Prot 16 g; Carbo 22 g; Fiber 1 g;
T Fat 9 g; Chol 33 mg; Sod 1066 mg.

Dietary Exchanges: Vegetable 3 1/2; Meat 1 1/2; Fat 1 1/2

SPINACH-FILLED TURKEY ROLL

1 1/2 pounds ground turkey
1/2 cup finely chopped onion
1/4 cup tomato sauce
2 slices bread, crumbled
2 eggs, beaten
1 teaspoon dry mustard
1/2 teaspoon oregano

1/4 teaspoon garlic powder
1 10-ounce package frozen
chopped spinach, thawed,
drained
1/2 cup shredded mozzarella
cheese
3/4 cup tomato sauce

Combine ground turkey, onion, 1/4 cup tomato sauce, bread crumbs, eggs, dry mustard, oregano and garlic powder in bowl; mix well. Pat into 8x12-inch rectangle on foil. Spread spinach over turkey; sprinkle with cheese. Roll from narrow side to enclose filling. Place seam side down in ungreased baking pan. Bake at 350 degrees for 1 hour. Let stand for 10 minutes. Heat 3/4 cup tomato sauce in saucepan. Slice turkey roll; serve with heated sauce.
Yield: 6 servings.

Approx Per Serving: Cal 250; Prot 32 g; Carbo 11 g; Fiber 1 g;
T Fat 9 g; Chol 164 mg; Sod 450 mg.

Dietary Exchanges: Vegetable 1; Bread/Starch 1/2; Meat 3 1/2; Fat 1/2

FISH

BAKED FISH MEDITERRANEAN

1 cup minced onion
1 clove of garlic, minced
1/2 cup chopped celery
2 tablespoons margarine
1   15-ounce can Italian-style
    tomato sauce

1/8 teaspoon cloves
1 bay leaf
1 1/2 cups shredded carrots
3/4 cup chicken broth
Salt and pepper to taste
2 pounds bluefish filets

Sauté onion, garlic and celery in margarine in skillet until tender but not brown. Add tomato sauce, cloves, bay leaf, carrots, broth, salt and pepper; mix well. Simmer, covered, for 30 minutes. Roll fish filets; secure with toothpicks. Arrange in greased shallow baking dish. Discard bay leaf; spoon sauce over filets. Bake at 350 degrees for 35 minutes or until fish flakes easily. Garnish with minced fresh parsley. Yield: 8 servings.

Approx Per Serving: Cal 207; Prot 26 g; Carbo 8 g; Fiber 1 g;
    T Fat 8 g; Chol <1 mg; Sod 466 mg.

Dietary Exchanges: Vegetable 1 1/2; Meat 3; Fat 1/2

BROILED GINGERED FISH

1 cup flour
1 teaspoon salt
1/2 teaspoon freshly ground
    pepper
4   6-ounce bluefish filets

4 teaspoons margarine
4 teaspoons minced
    gingerroot
2 lemons

Combine flour, salt and pepper in shallow dish. Coat filets with seasoned flour; place in oiled broiler pan. Dot with margarine; sprinkle with gingerroot. Slice lemons. Arrange lemon slices over filets, covering completely. Place under preheated broiler. Broil for 5 to 15 minutes or until fish flakes easily. Yield: 4 servings.

Approx Per Serving: Cal 372; Prot 39 g; Carbo 27 g; Fiber 1 g;
    T Fat 11 g; Chol 0 mg; Sod 676 mg.

Dietary Exchanges: Fruit 1/2; Bread/Starch 1 1/2; Meat 4 1/2; Fat 1

FISH CHOWDER

2 carrots, shredded
3 stalks celery, chopped
1½ cups water
2 bay leaves
1 pound halibut, cubed

2 cups mashed cooked
  potatoes
Salt and freshly ground
  pepper to taste

Combine carrots, celery, water and bay leaves in saucepan. Bring to a boil; reduce heat. Simmer, covered, for 10 minutes or until tender. Add halibut. Simmer, covered, until fish flakes easily. Add potatoes, salt and pepper; mix gently. Heat to serving temperature. Ladle into soup bowls. Garnish with finely shredded carrot and chopped green onions. Yield: 6 servings.

Approx Per Serving: Cal 152; Prot 18 g; Carbo 15 g; Fiber 1 g;
  T Fat 2 g; Chol 26 mg; Sod 280 mg.

Dietary Exchanges: Vegetable ½; Bread/Starch 1; Meat 2

FISH EN PAPILLOTE

2 tablespoons olive oil
6 6-ounce whitefish filets
1 teaspoon paprika

2 tablespoons lemon juice
Salt and freshly ground
  pepper to taste

Cut six 12x12-inch pieces baking parchment or foil. Rub each piece with 2 teaspoons olive oil. Place 1 filet on each piece. Sprinkle with paprika, lemon juice, salt and pepper. Bring opposite sides of parchment to center; fold over several times. Fold each end several times toward filet, sealing tightly. Place on baking sheet. Bake at 350 degrees for 30 minutes. Yield: 6 servings.

Approx Per Serving: Cal 334; Prot 21 g; Carbo 8 g; Fiber <1 g;
  T Fat 24 g; Chol 0 mg; Sod 265 mg.

Dietary Exchanges: Bread/Starch ½; Meat 3; Fat 3

☎ Select the thickness of fish filets for the recipe you intend to make. Thin filets may dry out too much when broiled, but in some recipes, thick filets may not be cooked through when the outer edges flake easily.

FISH PAPRIKA

4 onions, coarsely chopped
1 tablespoon margarine
2 teaspoons paprika
2 pounds flounder filets

Salt and pepper to taste
1 cup water
1/2 cup lowfat plain yogurt

Sauté onions in margarine in deep skillet for 10 minutes or until golden. Add paprika; mix well. Spread onions in even layer in skillet. Arrange filets over onions; sprinkle with salt and pepper. Pour water around edge of skillet. Bring to a boil; reduce heat. Simmer, covered, for 20 minutes or until fish flakes easily. Remove filets to serving plate; keep warm. Stir yogurt into onions and pan juices. Heat to serving temperature; do not boil. Spoon over filets. Yield: 6 servings.

Approx Per Serving: Cal 206; Prot 32 g; Carbo 9 g; Fiber 2 g;
    T Fat 4 g; Chol 83 mg; Sod 165 mg.

Dietary Exchanges: Vegetable 1 1/2; Meat 3; Fat 1/2

DILLED FLOUNDER

4 small tomatoes
4 4-ounce flounder filets
1/4 cup fine cracker crumbs
2 tablespoons Parmesan
  cheese
1 1/2 teaspoons chopped dill

1/4 teaspoon salt
1/2 teaspoon black pepper
1/8 teaspoon red pepper
1 tablespoon melted
  margarine

Slice each tomato into four 1/4-inch slices. Arrange tomato slices in baking dish sprayed with nonstick cooking spray. Arrange filets over tomatoes. Combine cracker crumbs, cheese, dill, salt, black pepper and red pepper in small bowl; mix well. Sprinkle over filets. Bake at 425 degrees for 13 minutes or until fish flakes easily. Yield: 4 servings.

Approx Per Serving: Cal 192; Prot 10 g; Carbo 17 g; Fiber 2 g;
    T Fat 10 g; Chol 4 mg; Sod 630 mg.

Dietary Exchanges: Vegetable 1; Bread/Starch 1; Meat 1; Fat 1 1/2

MICROWAVE ORANGE ROUGHY WITH LEMON SAUCE

6 4-ounce orange roughy
   filets
Salt and pepper to taste
1 tablespoon margarine
2 tablespoons flour

1/4 teaspoon salt
2/3 cup evaporated skim milk
1 tablespoon fresh lemon
   juice
1 teaspoon chopped chives

Arrange filets in 9-inch glass pie plate. Sprinkle with salt and pepper. Microwave, loosely covered with plastic wrap, on High for 4 to 6 minutes or until fish flakes easily, rotating pie plate once. Let stand, covered, for 5 minutes. Microwave margarine in 2-cup glass measure until melted. Blend in flour and 1/4 teaspoon salt. Stir in evaporated milk. Microwave on High for 3 to 4 minutes or until thickened and bubbly, stirring 2 or 3 times. Add lemon juice and chives; mix well. Spoon over filets. Yield: 6 servings.

Approx Per Serving: Cal 179; Prot 25 g; Carbo 4 g; Fiber <1 g;
    T Fat 7 g; Chol <1 mg; Sod 212 mg.

Dietary Exchanges: Meat 3; Fat 1/2

POACHED ORANGE ROUGHY

1 cup plain nonfat yogurt
2 tablespoons lemon juice
4 cups water

4 6-ounce orange roughy
   filets

Blend yogurt and lemon juice in small bowl. Chill, covered, until serving time. Bring water to a boil in large deep skillet. Add filets. Bring to a boil; reduce heat. Poach, covered, for 5 minutes. Turn filets over. Poach for 5 minutes longer or until fish flakes easily. Remove filets to serving platter. Serve with lemon-yogurt sauce and/or Picante Sauce (below). Yield: 4 servings.

Approx Per Serving: Cal 248; Prot 39 g; Carbo 5 g; Fiber <1 g;
    T Fat 7 g; Chol 1 mg; Sod 185 mg.

Dietary Exchanges: Milk 1/2; Meat 4 1/2

☎ For **Picante Sauce,** simmer one 15-ounce can tomatoes, 1 tablespoon olive oil, 1 tablespoon vinegar and 1/2 teaspoon crushed dried red peppers in saucepan for 10 minutes. Store in refrigerator.

BAKED SALMON PRIMAVERA

1 small onion, finely chopped
1 tablespoon margarine
3 cups shredded zucchini
1 cup shredded carrot
1/4 cup minced parsley

2 tablespoons minced fresh
  basil
4   4-ounce salmon steaks
1 teaspoon fresh lime juice
Salt and pepper to taste

Sauté onion in margarine in skillet until tender; remove from heat. Add zucchini, carrot, parsley and basil; mix lightly. Spoon into lightly greased 9x9-inch baking dish. Brush salmon with lime juice; arrange over vegetables. Sprinkle with salt and pepper. Bake, covered, at 350 degrees for 30 minutes. Bake, uncovered, for 10 minutes longer or until fish flakes easily. Yield: 4 servings.

Approx Per Serving: Cal 232; Prot 27 g; Carbo 8 g; Fiber 3 g;
    T Fat 10 g; Chol 45 mg; Sod 102 mg.

Dietary Exchanges: Vegetable 1 1/2; Meat 3; Fat 1/2

SALMON LOAF WITH CREAMY DIJON SAUCE

1   7-ounce can salmon,
    drained
2 cups chopped cooked
    potatoes
1/4 cup chopped celery
1/4 cup milk
1 egg, beaten
1/4 cup minced green onions

1/2 teaspoon grated lemon rind
Pepper to taste
2 tablespoons minced onion
1 tablespoon oil
1 tablespoon butter
1 tablespoon flour
1 cup milk
2 tablespoons Dijon mustard

Flake salmon in bowl. Add potatoes, celery, 1/4 cup milk, egg, green onions, lemon rind and pepper; mix well. Press into lightly greased loaf pan. Bake at 350 degrees for 25 minutes or until set. Sauté onion in mixture of oil and butter in skillet until tender. Blend in flour. Stir in 1 cup milk gradually. Cook until thickened, stirring constantly. Blend in mustard. Serve sauce with Salmon Loaf. Yield: 4 servings.

Approx Per Serving: Cal 266; Prot 16 g; Carbo 19 g; Fiber 1 g;
    T Fat 13 g; Chol 86 mg; Sod 466 mg.

Dietary Exchanges: Milk 1/2; Bread/Starch 1; Meat 1 1/2; Fat 2

POACHED SALMON

1/2 cup white wine
1 cup water
2 tablespoons wine vinegar
1/2 cup chopped celery leaves
1/4 bay leaf

7 peppercorns
1 teaspoon dillweed
5 whole allspice
8 6-ounce salmon steaks

Combine first 8 ingredients in skillet. Bring to a boil. Arrange salmon in skillet. Bring to a boil; reduce heat. Simmer, tightly covered, for 8 to 10 minutes or until fish flakes easily. Drain well; place on heated serving platter. Garnish with watercress or parsley. Yield: 8 servings.

Approx Per Serving: Cal 170; Prot 25 g; Carbo 1 g; Fiber <1 g;
    T Fat 6 g; Chol 31 mg; Sod 1083 mg.
    Nutritional information includes entire amount of poaching liquid.

Dietary Exchanges: Meat 3

MICROWAVE SALMON STEAKS WITH YOGURT SAUCE

4 4-ounce salmon filets
1 tablespoon fresh lime juice
2 teaspoons olive oil
1/2 teaspoon salt
1/4 teaspoon pepper
1/4 teaspoon cumin
1 plum tomato
2 teaspoons freshly grated
    gingerroot

1/4 teaspoon minced garlic
1/4 teaspoon cumin
3/4 cup plain nonfat yogurt
1 green onion, thinly sliced
1 tablespoon chopped mint
Red pepper sauce to taste
1/4 teaspoon salt
1/8 teaspoon freshly ground
    pepper

Arrange filets in glass pie plate. Combine next 5 ingredients in small bowl; mix well. Brush over filets. Let stand, tightly covered with plastic wrap, for 30 minutes. Turn back edge of plastic wrap. Microwave on High for 3 to 4 minutes or until opaque, turning pie plate once. Let stand, covered, for 2 minutes. Remove to serving plate. Seed and chop tomato; place in small glass bowl. Add ginger, garlic and cumin. Microwave on High for 30 seconds. Add remaining ingredients; mix well. Let stand for several minutes. Spoon sauce over salmon. Garnish with lime wedges and mint. Yield: 4 servings.

Approx Per Serving: Cal 219; Prot 28 g; Carbo 5 g; Fiber <1 g;
    T Fat 9 g; Chol 46 mg; Sod 455 mg.

Dietary Exchanges: Milk 1/2; Vegetable 1/2; Meat 3; Fat 1/2

BAKED SWORDFISH WITH VEGETABLES

2 pounds fresh swordfish
  steaks
1/2 cup sliced green onions
11/2 cups sliced fresh
  mushrooms
1 2-ounce jar chopped
  pimento, drained

1 medium tomato, chopped
1/4 cup chopped green bell
  pepper
2 tablespoons lemon juice
1/4 teaspoon salt
1/8 teaspoon pepper

Cut swordfish into 8 serving pieces. Sprinkle green onions into of 8x12-inch baking dish sprayed with nonstick cooking spray. Arrange swordfish in prepared dish. Combine mushrooms, pimento, tomato and green pepper in bowl; toss lightly. Spoon over swordfish. Sprinkle lemon juice, salt and pepper over top. Bake, covered, at 350 degrees for 30 minutes or until fish flakes easily.
Yield: 8 servings.

Approx Per Serving: Cal 151; Prot 24 g; Carbo 2 g; Fiber <1 g;
  T Fat 5 g; Chol 46 mg; Sod 168 mg.

Dietary Exchanges: Vegetable 1/2; Meat 3

OVEN-FRIED TROUT

1 pound trout filets
1 tablespoon olive oil
1/4 teaspoon salt substitute

1/8 teaspoon garlic powder
1/8 teaspoon pepper
1/3 cup cornflake crumbs

Rinse trout; pat dry. Brush with olive oil; sprinkle with salt substitute, garlic powder and pepper. Coat with cornflake crumbs. Arrange in baking pan sprayed with nonstick cooking spray. Bake, uncovered, at 500 degrees for 10 minutes or until fish flakes easily. Remove carefully to serving platter. Garnish with lemon slices and parsley. Yield: 4 servings.

Approx Per Serving: Cal 190; Prot 24 g; Carbo 5 g; Fiber <1 g;
  T Fat 7 g; Chol 66 mg; Sod 101 mg.

Dietary Exchanges: Bread/Starch 1/2; Meat 3; Fat 1/2

QUICK AND EASY BARBECUED TUNA FOR ONE

4 ounces drained water-pack tuna
1/4 teaspoon chili powder
1 tablespoon Worcestershire sauce
1 tablespoon dry mustard
1 tablespoon instant onion flakes
1/2 cup tomato juice

Flake tuna in small saucepan. Add chili powder, Worcestershire sauce, dry mustard, onion flakes and tomato juice; mix well. Simmer for 5 minutes, stirring frequently. Serve over toast or English muffin. Yield: 1 serving.

Approx Per Serving: Cal 188; Prot 32 g; Carbo 8 g; Fiber 1 g;
   T Fat 3 g; Chol 47 mg; Sod 1032 mg.

Dietary Exchanges: Vegetable 1; Meat 3½

TUNA BURGERS

1   6-ounce can water-pack tuna, drained
1/2 cup soft bread crumbs
1/2 cup finely chopped celery
2 tablespoons minced onion
1/3 cup mayonnaise-type salad dressing
2 tablespoons chili sauce
1 teaspoon lemon juice

Flake tuna in bowl. Add bread crumbs, celery and onion; toss until mixed. Blend salad dressing, chili sauce and lemon juice in small bowl. Add to tuna mixture; mix well. Shape into 5 patties. Place in preheated lightly oiled skillet. Cook over low to medium heat for 5 minutes on each side or until light brown. Serve plain or on buns with lettuce and tomato. Yield: 5 servings.

Approx Per Serving: Cal 127; Prot 10 g; Carbo 8 g; Fiber <1 g;
   T Fat 6 g; Chol 18 mg; Sod 357 mg.

Dietary Exchanges: Meat 1; Fat 1½

RED CLAM SPAGHETTI

2 cloves of garlic, minced
1 tablespoon olive oil
1 tablespoon flour
1 6-ounce can minced clams
2 tablespoons parsley flakes

1 20-ounce can Italian tomatoes, mashed
1 12-ounce package spaghetti

Sauté garlic in olive oil in skillet. Stir in flour. Cook until flour is light brown, stirring constantly. Add undrained clams, parsley and tomatoes; mix well. Bring to a boil; reduce heat. Simmer for 15 minutes. Cook spaghetti using package directions. Drain; rinse under hot running water and drain well. Place in large bowl. Pour half the sauce over spaghetti; toss until coated. Place on large serving plate. Ladle remaining sauce over top. Yield: 6 servings.

Approx Per Serving: Cal 272; Prot 11 g; Carbo 49 g; Fiber 3 g;
   T Fat 4 g; Chol 18 mg; Sod 170 mg.

Dietary Exchanges: Vegetable 1; Bread/Starch 3½; Meat ½; Fat ½

CRAB MEAT PUFF

1 medium onion, finely chopped
8 ounces fresh mushrooms, thinly sliced
¼ cup margarine
¼ cup flour
1½ cups light cream

1 pound crab meat, flaked
¼ cup Sherry
Juice of ½ lemon
½ teaspoon paprika
Salt and pepper to taste
6 tablespoons dry bread crumbs

Sauté onion and mushrooms in margarine in skillet. Sprinkle with flour. Cook for 3 minutes, stirring constantly. Stir in cream. Cook until thickened, stirring constantly. Add crab meat, Sherry, lemon juice, paprika, salt and pepper; mix gently. Spoon into 6 baking shells. Sprinkle with bread crumbs. Bake at 375 degrees for 10 minutes or until golden brown and bubbly. Yield: 6 servings.

Approx Per Serving: Cal 360; Prot 14 g; Carbo 12 g; Fiber 1 g;
   T Fat 28 g; Chol 127 mg; Sod 413 mg.

Dietary Exchanges: Vegetable 1; Bread/Starch ½; Meat 1½; Fat 6

NO-CRUST CRAB MEAT QUICHE

4 ounces crab meat, flaked
1 cup shredded Cheddar
  cheese
1/4 cup chopped green onions
4 eggs, beaten

1 cup evaporated skim milk
1/2 teaspoon salt
1/2 teaspoon dry mustard
1/8 teaspoon pepper
Paprika to taste

Spray 8-inch pie plate with nonstick cooking spray. Layer crab meat, cheese and green onions in pie plate. Beat eggs with evaporated skim milk in bowl. Mix in salt, dry mustard and pepper. Pour into pie plate. Sprinkle with paprika. Bake at 400 degrees for 30 minutes or until set. Let stand for 5 minutes. May substitute tuna or chicken for crab meat. May substitute egg substitute for eggs. Yield: 4 servings.

Approx Per Serving: Cal 266; Prot 22 g; Carbo 8 g; Fiber <1 g;
    T Fat 16 g; Chol 329 mg; Sod 675 mg.

Dietary Exchanges: Milk 1/2; Meat 21/2; Fat 2

STIR-FRY CRAB DELIGHT

8 ounces crab meat, flaked
1 10-ounce package frozen
  oriental-style vegetables

1/8 teaspoon garlic powder
1/8 teaspoon ginger
2 cups hot cooked rice

Combine crab meat, vegetables, garlic powder and ginger in preheated skillet over medium heat. Add a small amount of water. Cook, covered, for 2 minutes or until vegetables thaw. Stir-fry for 2 minutes or until vegetables are tender-crisp. Serve over hot cooked rice with soy sauce. Yield: 4 servings.

Approx Per Serving: Cal 180; Prot 12 g; Carbo 30 g; Fiber 3 g;
    T Fat 1 g; Chol 45 mg; Sod 254 mg.

Dietary Exchanges: Vegetable 11/2; Bread/Starch 11/2; Meat 1

☎ Stir-frying is a quick, nutritious way to prepare meat, chicken, seafood and vegetables. Spray the skillet or wok with vegetable cooking spray to further reduce calories. Cut ingredients into uniform pieces for even cooking.

SCALLOPS THERMIDOR

1 cup sliced fresh mushrooms
1/4 cup margarine
1/4 cup flour
1/2 teaspoon dry mustard
Salt and cayenne pepper to
  taste
2 cups milk
1 pound scallops
2 tablespoons minced fresh
  parsley
1/4 cup Parmesan cheese
Paprika to taste

Sauté mushrooms in margarine in skillet until tender. Add flour, dry mustard, salt and cayenne pepper; mix well. Stir in milk gradually. Cook until thickened, stirring constantly. Cut large scallops into halves. Stir scallops and parsley into sauce. Spoon into greased 2-quart casserole. Sprinkle with Parmesan cheese and paprika. Bake at 400 degrees for 15 minutes or until bubbly and golden brown. Yield: 4 servings.

Approx Per Serving: Cal 318; Prot 23 g; Carbo 15 g; Fiber <1 g;
    T Fat 18 g; Chol 51 mg; Sod 455 mg.

Dietary Exchanges: Milk 1/2; Bread/Starch 1/2; Meat 21/2; Fat 31/2

SCALLOPS SAINT JACQUES

11/2 cups sliced fresh
  mushrooms
1/4 cup minced onion
2 tablespoons margarine
8 ounces scallops
1/4 cup margarine
3 tablespoons flour
1/4 teaspoon dry mustard
1/2 teaspoon grated lemon rind
1/2 teaspoon horseradish
  powder
2 cups light cream
8 ounces small peeled
  shrimp, cooked
4 ounces crab meat, flaked
2 tablespoons dry Sherry
1/4 cup dry bread crumbs

Sauté mushrooms and onion in 2 tablespoons margarine in skillet until tender; remove with slotted spoon. Cut scallops into bite-sized pieces; add to pan juices in skillet. Sauté for 3 minutes; set aside. Melt 1/4 cup margarine in saucepan. Blend in flour, dry mustard, lemon rind and horseradish. Stir in cream gradually. Cook until thickened, stirring constantly. Add sautéed mushrooms, scallops, shrimp, crab meat and Sherry; mix well. Spoon into baking shells or ramekins. Sprinkle with bread crumbs. Bake at 400 degrees for 10 minutes. Broil until light brown. Yield: 10 servings.

Approx Per Serving: Cal 253; Prot 10 g; Carbo 6 g; Fiber <1 g;
    T Fat 21 g; Chol 104 mg; Sod 213 mg.

Dietary Exchanges: Meat 1; Fat 41/2

LEMON-MARINATED SHRIMP KABOBS

2½ pounds large fresh shrimp
½ cup lemon juice
⅓ cup reduced-calorie Italian salad dressing
¼ cup reduced-sodium soy sauce

¼ cup water
3 tablespoons minced fresh parsley
3 tablespoons minced onion
1 clove of garlic, crushed
½ teaspoon pepper

Peel and devein shrimp; place in large shallow dish. Combine lemon juice, salad dressing, soy sauce, water, parsley, onion, garlic and pepper in small bowl; mix well. Pour over shrimp. Marinate, covered, in refrigerator for 4 hours. Drain, reserving marinade. Thread shrimp onto skewers. Arrange on grill or rack in broiler pan. Broil 5 to 6 inches from medium heat source for 3 to 4 minutes on each side, basting frequently with reserved marinade. Yield: 6 servings.

Approx Per Serving: Cal 176; Prot 33 g; Carbo 3 g; Fiber <1 g;
    T Fat 3 g; Chol 296 mg; Sod 956 mg.
    Nutritional information includes entire amount of marinade.

Dietary Exchanges: Meat 3½; Fat ½

SHRIMP CREOLE OVER BULGUR WHEAT

1 cup bulgur wheat
1⅔ cups water
1 green bell pepper, chopped
1 cup chopped onion
½ cup chopped celery
1 tablespoon olive oil
2 cloves of garlic, minced
1 tablespoon minced parsley

⅛ teaspoon (scant) cayenne pepper
1 bay leaf
1   28-ounce can tomatoes, chopped
1 pound fresh shrimp, peeled, deveined

Combine bulgur and water in saucepan. Bring to a boil; cover and reduce heat. Simmer for 15 minutes or until water is absorbed. Sauté green pepper, onion and celery in olive oil until tender. Stir in garlic, parsley, cayenne pepper and bay leaf. Add tomatoes; mix well. Simmer, covered, for 30 minutes. Add shrimp. Cook for 5 to 10 minutes or until shrimp are pink. Discard bay leaf. Serve immediately over hot bulgur. Bulgur may be cooked, stored in plastic bag in freezer and microwaved for 3 to 5 minutes to reheat. Yield: 4 servings.

Approx Per Serving: Cal 224; Prot 17 g; Carbo 32 g; Fiber 2 g;
    T Fat 4 g; Chol 118 mg; Sod 360 mg.

Dietary Exchanges: Vegetable 1½; Bread/Starch 1½; Meat 1½; Fat ½

EASY SHRIMP CREOLE

1 medium onion, chopped
1 small green bell pepper,
  chopped
1 tablespoon olive oil
1 8-ounce can tomato sauce
1 10-ounce can Ro-Tel
  tomatoes with chilies

1 teaspoon minced garlic
Pepper to taste
1 pound fresh shrimp,
  peeled, deveined
1¹/₂ cups hot cooked rice

Sauté onion and green pepper in olive oil in skillet until tender-crisp. Add tomato sauce, Ro-Tel tomatoes, garlic and pepper. Simmer until heated through, stirring occasionally. Add shrimp. Simmer until shrimp turn pink. Serve over hot cooked rice. Yield: 3 servings.

Approx Per Serving: Cal 346; Prot 36 g; Carbo 35 g; Fiber 3 g;
  T Fat 7 g; Chol 295 mg; Sod 952 mg.

Dietary Exchanges: Vegetable 2¹/₂; Bread 1¹/₂; Meat 3¹/₂; Fat 1

PEKING SHRIMP

¹/₄ cup dark corn syrup
¹/₄ cup water
2 tablespoons reduced-
  sodium soy sauce
2 tablespoons Sherry
1 clove of garlic, minced
1 tablespoon cornstarch

¹/₄ teaspoon ginger
2 tablespoons corn oil
1 pound peeled shrimp
1 cup chopped green bell
  pepper
2 tomatoes, chopped
2 cups hot cooked rice

Combine corn syrup, water, soy sauce, Sherry, garlic, cornstarch and ginger in small bowl; mix well and set aside. Heat corn oil in skillet over medium heat. Add shrimp. Stir-fry until shrimp are pink. Stir in soy sauce mixture and green pepper. Cook over high heat for 2 minutes, stirring constantly. Stir in tomato. Serve over hot cooked rice. Yield: 4 servings.

Approx Per Serving: Cal 342; Prot 23 g; Carbo 42 g; Fiber 2 g;
  T Fat 8 g; Chol 177 mg; Sod 611 mg.

Dietary Exchanges: Vegetable ¹/₂; Bread/Starch 1¹/₂; Meat 2; Fat 1¹/₂

1937

CAJUN SEAFOOD SAUTÉ

1/4 cup chopped green onions
1 clove of garlic, minced
1 tablespoon margarine
1 cup small peeled shrimp
1/2 teaspoon oregano
1/2 teaspoon thyme
1/2 teaspoon pepper

1/4 teaspoon cayenne pepper
2 tablespoons Dijon mustard
1/2 cup sliced fresh
  mushrooms
1 cup flaked crab meat
1/3 cup white wine
2 cups hot cooked rice

Sauté green onions and garlic in margarine in skillet for 1 minute. Add shrimp. Sauté until shrimp turn pink. Stir in seasonings. Sauté for 30 seconds. Add mustard and mushrooms. Sauté for 30 seconds. Add crab meat. Sauté for 30 seconds. Stir in wine. Cook for 1 minute. Serve over rice. Yield: 4 servings.

Approx Per Serving: Cal 207; Prot 15 g; Carbo 22 g; Fiber 1 g;
    T Fat 4 g; Chol 83 mg; Sod 334 mg.

Dietary Exchanges: Bread 1 1/2; Meat 1 1/2; Fat 1/2

SEAFOOD LASAGNA

1 cup chopped onion
2 tablespoons margarine
8 ounces cream cheese,
  softened
1 1/2 cups cream-style cottage
  cheese
1 egg, beaten
2 teaspoons basil
Salt and pepper to taste
1/3 cup dry white wine

2 10-ounce cans cream of
  mushroom soup
1 soup can milk
1 pound peeled shrimp,
  cooked
1 7-ounce can crab meat,
  drained, flaked
8 lasagna noodles, cooked
1/4 cup Parmesan cheese
1/2 shredded Cheddar cheese

Sauté onion in margarine in skillet; remove from heat. Add cream cheese; stir until melted. Add cottage cheese, egg and seasonings; mix well. Blend wine, soup and milk in bowl. Add shrimp and crab meat; mix well. Layer noodles, cottage cheese mixture and seafood mixture 1/2 at a time in greased 9x13-inch baking dish. Sprinkle Parmesan cheese over top. Bake at 350 degrees for 45 minutes. Top with Cheddar cheese. Bake for 3 minutes longer. Let stand for 15 minutes. Yield: 12 servings.

Approx Per Serving: Cal 338; Prot 21 g; Carbo 21 g; Fiber <1 g
    T Fat 18 g; Chol 134 mg; Sod 818 mg.

Dietary Exchanges: Bread/Starch 2; Meat 2; Fat 4 1/2

MICROWAVE SEAFOOD STEW

1/2 cup thinly sliced onion
2 teaspoons olive oil
1/2 teaspoon minced garlic
1 3-inch strip orange rind
1 tablespoon fresh thyme
1 whole allspice
1 14-ounce can plum
   tomatoes, sieved

1 8-ounce bottle of clam
   juice
Salt, pepper and red pepper
   flakes to taste
12 mussels
8 ounces cod filet
4 jumbo shrimp, peeled,
   deveined

Combine onion, oil, garlic, orange rind, thyme and allspice in 3-quart glass casserole. Microwave, covered, on High for 4 minutes. Stir in tomatoes, clam juice, salt, pepper and red pepper flakes. Microwave for 7 minutes, stirring once. Scrub mussels. Arrange around edge of casserole. Microwave, covered, for 3 minutes. Remove open mussels to covered bowl. Microwave, covered, for 1 to 2 minutes longer, removing mussels when open. Discard any unopened mussels. Cut cod into 4 pieces. Add cod and shrimp to casserole. Microwave, covered, for 2 1/2 to 3 minutes or until fish flakes easily and shrimp are pink. Divide mussels among 4 large soup bowls; add shrimp and cod. Ladle broth over seafood. Serve immediately.
Yield: 4 servings.

Approx Per Serving: Cal 166; Prot 22 g; Carbo 6 g; Fiber 1 g;
   T Fat 6 g; Chol 55 mg; Sod 333 mg.

Dietary Exchanges: Vegetable 1; Meat 2 1/2; Fat 1/2

☎ Some fish is "leaner" than others:

- "Lean" fish include: bluefish, ocean catfish, cod, flounder, grouper, haddock, halibut, ocean perch, red snapper, sole, swordfish and turbot.

- "Fat" fish include: amberjack, carp, freshwater catfish, mackerel, mullet, salmon, tuna and whitefish.

- The redder the salmon, the higher the oil content.

- Try imitation shellfish products (surimi) that are made from fish and are lower in cholesterol and fat.

Vegetables
and Side Dishes

VEGETABLES AND SIDE DISHES

MICROWAVE ASPARAGUS AND MUSHROOMS

1 tablespoon corn oil
  margarine
8 ounces fresh asparagus,
  cut into 2-inch pieces
1/2 teaspoon basil
Pepper to taste

8 ounces fresh mushrooms,
  sliced
1 medium tomato, cut into
  wedges
Salt to taste

Microwave margarine on High in 1 1/2-quart dish for 30 seconds. Add asparagus, basil and pepper; mix well. Microwave, covered, for 3 minutes. Add mushrooms. Microwave, covered, for 3 minutes. Add tomato. Microwave, covered, for 1 1/2 minutes. Season with salt. Let stand, covered, for 3 minutes. Yield: 4 servings.

Approx Per Serving: Cal 60; Prot 3 g; Carbo 6 g; Fiber 2 g;
   T Fat 3 g; Chol 0 mg; Sod 40 mg.

Dietary Exchanges: Vegetable 1 1/2; Fat 1/2

SPICED ASPARAGUS VINAIGRETTE

2/3 cup white vinegar
1/2 cup water
1/2 cup sugar
3 cinnamon sticks

1 teaspoon whole cloves
1 teaspoon celery seed
2 pounds fresh asparagus
  spears, cooked, drained

Bring vinegar, water, sugar, cinnamon sticks, cloves and celery seed to a boil in medium saucepan over medium-high heat. Pour over asparagus in shallow dish. Marinate, covered, in refrigerator overnight. Drain at serving time. May serve hot or cold. May substitute two 16-ounce cans asparagus spears for fresh asparagus. Yield: 6 servings.

Approx Per Serving: Cal 97; Prot 4 g; Carbo 24 g; Fiber 2 g;
   T Fat <1 g; Chol 0 mg; Sod 7 mg.
   Nutritional information includes entire amount of marinade.

Dietary Exchanges: Vegetable 1 1/2

BEANS AND RICE

1 large onion
4 whole cloves
2 cups dried beans
4 cups bouillon
2 dried red peppers
1 bay leaf
1 teaspoon salt

1/2 teaspoon pepper
3 1/2 cups bouillon
2 cups uncooked brown rice
1 teaspoon chopped chives
1/2 green bell pepper, minced
1/2 cup shredded Cheddar
  cheese

Stud onion with cloves. Combine with beans and 4 cups bouillon in large saucepan. Let stand overnight. Add red peppers, bay leaf, salt and pepper to beans. Add enough water to cover beans. Bring to a boil; reduce heat. Simmer for 4 hours or until tender. Remove bay leaf. Bring 3 1/2 cups bouillon to a boil in saucepan. Add rice, chives and green pepper. Bring to a boil; reduce heat. Simmer, covered, for 40 minutes or until rice is tender; do not stir. Serve beans over rice. Top with cheese. Yield: 8 servings.

Approx Per Serving: Cal 393; Prot 21 g; Carbo 66 g; Fiber 12 g;
   T Fat 5 g; Chol 8 mg; Sod 1031 mg.

Dietary Exchanges: Vegetable 1/2; Bread/Starch 4 1/2; Meat 1 1/2; Fat 1/2

GREEN BEANS WITH GARLIC

1 1/2 pounds young tender
  green beans
2 tablespoons dry bread
  crumbs
2 tablespoons chopped leaf
  parsley

6 cloves of garlic, minced
Salt and freshly ground
  pepper to taste
2 tablespoons extra-virgin
  olive oil
2 tablespoons margarine

Steam green beans in saucepan for 6 to 8 minutes or until tender-crisp; drain. Rinse with ice water. Sauté bread crumbs, parsley, garlic, salt and pepper in olive oil in skillet over low heat for 1 minute. Add margarine and green beans. Cook until heated through. Serve immediately. Yield: 6 servings.

Approx Per Serving: Cal 126; Prot 3 g; Carbo 12 g; Fiber 2 g;
   T Fat 9 g; Chol 0 mg; Sod 65 mg.

Dietary Exchanges: Vegetable 2; Fat 2

GREEN BEANS AND TOMATOES

1 medium onion, finely
  chopped
2 tablespoons oil
1 16-ounce can stewed
  tomatoes

1 tablespoon sugar
1 10-ounce package frozen
  green beans
Salt and pepper to taste

Sauté onion in oil in saucepan until golden brown. Add tomatoes. Bring to a boil. Add sugar and green beans. Cook, covered, until green beans are tender. Season with salt and pepper. Yield: 6 servings.

Approx Per Serving: Cal 81; Prot 2 g; Carbo 9 g; Fiber 2 g;
    T Fat 5 g; Chol 0 mg; Sod 242 mg.

Dietary Exchanges: Vegetable 1½; Fat 1

BROCCOLI AND CHEESE CASSEROLE

1 small onion, chopped
1 tablespoon water
1 10-ounce package frozen
  chopped broccoli
1 7-ounce package long
  grain and wild rice with
  mushrooms mix

1 tablespoon corn oil
  margarine
¼ teaspoon salt
2 tablespoons flour
1 cup evaporated skim milk
3 ounces American cheese,
  shredded

Cook onion in water in skillet until transparent. Microwave broccoli using package directions for 6 minutes; drain. Prepare rice using package directions, omitting 2 teaspoons margarine. Melt margarine in large saucepan; remove from heat. Blend in salt and flour. Add milk gradually, stirring to mix well. Cook until thickened, stirring constantly. Stir in cheese until melted. Add onion, broccoli and rice; mix well. Spoon into 1½-quart baking dish sprayed with nonstick cooking spray. Bake at 350 degrees for 30 minutes. Yield: 8 servings.

Approx Per Serving: Cal 189; Prot 8 g; Carbo 28 g; Fiber 2 g;
    T Fat 5 g; Chol 12 mg; Sod 278 mg.

Dietary Exchanges: Milk ½; Vegetable ½; Bread/Starch 1½; Meat ½; Fat 1

BAKED SWEET AND SOUR BRUSSELS SPROUTS

1 10-ounce package frozen
   Brussels sprouts
2 tablespoons oil
¼ cup cider vinegar

1 tablespoon sugar
Salt and pepper to taste
2 tablespoons Parmesan
   cheese

Cook Brussels sprouts using package directions; drain. Arrange in 9x13-inch baking dish. Combine oil, vinegar, sugar, salt and pepper in small bowl; mix well. Pour over Brussels sprouts. Sprinkle with cheese. Bake, covered, at 350 degrees for 15 minutes. May substitute fresh Brussels sprouts for frozen. Yield: 4 servings.

Approx Per Serving: Cal 115; Prot 4 g; Carbo 10 g; Fiber 2 g;
   T Fat 8 g; Chol 2 mg; Sod 75 mg.

Dietary Exchanges: Vegetable 1½; Meat ½; Fat 1½

JAPANESE CABBAGE

½ cup chicken broth
2 tablespoons soy sauce
4 cups thinly sliced cabbage

1 cup sliced celery
1 tablespoon chopped green
   onion

Bring chicken broth and soy sauce to a boil in large skillet. Add cabbage, celery and green onion. Cook over high heat for 5 minutes or until tender-crisp, turning vegetables frequently with pancake turner; do not overcook. Yield: 4 servings.

Approx Per Serving: Cal 37; Prot 3 g; Carbo 7 g; Fiber 2 g;
   T Fat <1 g; Chol <1 mg; Sod 654 mg.

Dietary Exchanges: Vegetable 1

☎ Make a **Skim Milk White Sauce** by blending 2 tablespoons melted margarine with 2 tablespoons flour and white pepper to taste. Stir in 1 cup skim milk and cook until thickened, stirring constantly. Use as a sauce for vegetables or as a substitute for canned soups in casseroles.

PENNSYLVANIA RED CABBAGE

1 large onion, finely chopped
2 tablespoons shortening
2 apples, peeled, thinly sliced
1 cup water
1/2 cup red wine vinegar
2 tablespoons sugar

Salt and pepper to taste
1 bay leaf
1 medium head red cabbage,
  shredded
1 tablespoon flour

Sauté onion in shortening in large skillet for 3 to 4 minutes. Add apples. Cook for several minutes. Stir in water, vinegar, sugar, salt, pepper and bay leaf. Bring to a boil. Add cabbage. Simmer, tightly covered, for 40 to 50 minutes or until cabbage is tender, stirring occasionally. Remove bay leaf. Stir in flour. Cook until thickened, stirring constantly. Serve with pork, duck or other game. Yield: 8 servings.

Approx Per Serving: Cal 80; Prot 1 g; Carbo 14 g; Fiber 2 g;
    T Fat 3 g; Chol 0 mg; Sod 4 mg.

Dietary Exchanges: Vegetable 1/2; Fruit 1/2; Fat 1/2

COMPANY CARROTS

2 cups shredded carrots
2 cups finely sliced green
  onions
1/4 cup margarine

1/4 cup chicken broth
3/4 teaspoon fennel
3 tablespoons Grand Marnier

Stir-fry carrots and green onions in margarine in large skillet until green onions are transparent. Add chicken broth; mix well. Simmer, covered, until carrots are tender-crisp. Add fennel. Stir in Grand Marnier just before serving. Garnish with chopped parsley. May substitute nutmeg or anise for fennel and Triple Sec, Cointreau or orange juice for Grand Marnier. Yield: 6 servings.

Approx Per Serving: Cal 112; Prot 1 g; Carbo 7 g; Fiber 1 g;
    T Fat 8 g; Chol <1 mg; Sod 135 mg.

Dietary Exchanges: Vegetable 1/2; Fat 1 1/2

GINGER CARROTS

1/4 cup orange juice
1/4 cup chicken broth
1 teaspoon corn oil margarine
Grated rind of 1 lemon
1/2 cup sugar

1/2 teaspoon ginger
5 whole cloves
1 bunch baby carrots,
   trimmed

Bring orange juice, chicken broth, margarine, lemon rind, sugar, ginger and cloves to a boil in saucepan; reduce heat. Simmer for 10 minutes. Add carrots. Simmer until carrots are tender-crisp. Yield: 4 servings.

Approx Per Serving: Cal 115; Prot 1 g; Carbo 28 g; Fiber <1 g;
   T Fat 1 g; Chol <1 mg; Sod 71 mg.

Dietary Exchanges: Fat 1/2

HERBED CORN ON THE COB

3 tablespoons minced fresh
   dill or 1 tablespoon dried
   dill
3 tablespoons minced fresh
   thyme or 1 tablespoon
   dried thyme

1 tablespoon water
1 tablespoon safflower oil
1 clove of garlic, minced
4 ears fresh corn

Combine dill, thyme, water, oil and garlic in small bowl; mix well. Brush on corn. Wrap each ear individually in foil. Bake at 450 degrees for 25 minutes, turning several times. Yield: 4 servings.

Approx Per Serving: Cal 119; Prot 3 g; Carbo 21 g; Fiber 7 g;
   T Fat 4 g; Chol 0 mg; Sod 16 mg.

Dietary Exchanges: Bread/Starch 1 1/2; Fat 1/2

☎ Serve vegetables with **Dijon Yogurt** made of 4 ounces plain nonfat yogurt and 2 tablespoons Dijon mustard.

EGGPLANT CASSEROLE

1 medium onion, chopped
1 small green bell pepper,
  chopped
1/3 cup olive oil
1 medium eggplant, chopped
2 tomatoes, chopped
1 4-ounce can sliced
  mushrooms
1/4 teaspoon garlic powder

1/2 teaspoon oregano
Seasoned salt and salt
  to taste
Pepper to taste
1 cup rice, cooked
1 cup shredded sharp
  Cheddar cheese
1 cup bread crumbs

Sauté onion and green pepper in olive oil in saucepan until tender. Add eggplant, tomatoes, mushrooms, garlic powder, oregano, seasoned salt, salt and pepper; mix well. Simmer for 15 to 20 minutes or to desired consistency. Alternate layers of eggplant mixture and rice in greased 2-quart baking dish, beginning and ending with eggplant. Top with mixture of cheese and bread crumbs. Bake at 350 degrees for 30 minutes. Yield: 10 servings.

Approx Per Serving: Cal 240; Prot 6 g; Carbo 28 g; Fiber 2 g;
    T Fat 12 g; Chol 12 mg; Sod 148 mg.

Dietary Exchanges: Vegetable 1; Bread/Starch 1 1/2; Meat 1/2; Fat 2

MUSHROOMS AND ONIONS

1 medium onion, sliced
1 tablespoon oil

1 8-ounce can sliced
  mushrooms, drained

Sauté onion in oil in skillet until transparent. Add mushrooms. Cook until heated through. Serve with steaks or prime rib. Yield: 4 servings.

Approx Per Serving: Cal 58; Prot 2 g; Carbo 6 g; Fiber 2 g;
    T Fat 4 g; Chol 0 mg; Sod 1 mg.

Dietary Exchanges: Vegetable 1; Fat 1/2

OKRA AND TOMATOES

2 medium onions, chopped
3 tablespoons olive oil
1   10-ounce package frozen
    chopped okra
1 green bell pepper, chopped
2   16-ounce cans tomatoes,
    drained

1/2 teaspoon cumin seed
1/2 teaspoon garlic powder
1 teaspoon Italian seasoning
Tabasco sauce to taste

Sauté onions in olive oil in large skillet until tender. Add okra and green pepper. Sauté until tender; push to 1 side of skillet. Add tomatoes; cover skillet. Bring to a simmer; mix well. Sprinkle with cumin, garlic powder, Italian seasoning and Tabasco sauce. Simmer, covered, for 30 minutes or until most of the liquid has been reduced. May serve over brown or wild rice or with shrimp. Flavor improves with reheating. May use fresh okra in season. Yield: 6 servings.

Approx Per Serving: Cal 125; Prot 3 g; Carbo 14 g; Fiber 3 g;
    T Fat 7 g; Chol 0 mg; Sod 250 mg.

Dietary Exchanges: Vegetable 2 1/2; Fat 1 1/2

ONIONS PARMESAN

8 medium onions, sliced
1/4 cup margarine

1/2 cup Parmesan cheese

Sauté onions in margarine in skillet for 10 to 12 minutes. Place in 2 1/2-quart baking dish. Sprinkle with cheese. Broil 5 inches from heat until cheese melts. Yield: 6 servings.

Approx Per Serving: Cal 178; Prot 6 g; Carbo 16 g; Fiber 4 g;
    T Fat 11 g; Chol 7 mg; Sod 250 mg.

Dietary Exchanges: Vegetable 3; Meat 1/2; Fat 2

PARSNIPS IN ORANGE SAUCE

12 small parsnips, cooked
2 tablespoons light brown
  sugar
2 tablespoons light corn
  syrup

1/2 cup orange juice
Salt and paprika to taste
1 tablespoon corn oil
  margarine
Freshly grated orange rind

Arrange parsnips in greased shallow 8x12-inch baking dish. Combine brown sugar, corn syrup, orange juice, salt and paprika in small bowl; mix well. Pour over parsnips. Dot with margarine; sprinkle with orange rind. Bake at 400 degrees for 20 minutes. Yield: 6 servings.

Approx Per Serving: Cal 129; Prot 1 g; Carbo 27 g; Fiber <1 g;
  T Fat 2 g; Chol 0 mg; Sod 38 mg.

Dietary Exchanges: Bread/Starch 1; Fat 1/2

PARTY PEAS

1 10-ounce package frozen
  peas
1/3 cup chopped onion
2 tablespoons margarine

1 teaspoon sugar
1 3-ounce can sliced
  mushrooms, drained
Salt and pepper to taste

Cook peas using package directions; drain. Sauté onion in margarine in saucepan until tender; do not brown. Stir in peas, sugar and mushrooms. Season with salt and pepper. Cook, covered, over low heat, until heated through. Yield: 4 servings.

Approx Per Serving: Cal 120; Prot 4 g; Carbo 13 g; Fiber 3 g;
  T Fat 6 g; Chol 0 mg; Sod 128 mg.

Dietary Exchanges: Vegetable 1/2; Bread/Starch 1; Fat 1 1/2

MICROWAVE FANCY BAKED POTATOES

4 large baking potatoes
2 medium onions, sliced

Salt and pepper to taste

Slice 4 crosswise cuts in each potato, leaving bottom intact. Place 1 onion slice in each cut. Sprinkle with salt and pepper; spray with nonstick cooking spray. Wrap individually in plastic wrap. Microwave on High for 10 minutes, rearranging potatoes after 5 minutes. Let stand, wrapped, for 10 minutes longer. Top with Yogurt Butter Spread (page 149) or Dijon Yogurt (page 139). Yield: 4 servings.

Approx Per Serving: Cal 172; Prot 4 g; Carbo 39 g; Fiber 5 g;
T Fat <1 g; Chol 0 mg; Sod 10 mg.

Dietary Exchanges: Vegetable 1; Bread/Starch 2

POTATOES PAPRIKASH

4 medium potatoes, coarsely
  chopped
1 green bell pepper, chopped
1 onion, chopped

1 tablespoon margarine
1 tablespoon chopped parsley
Salt, pepper and paprika to
  taste

Simmer potatoes in water to just cover in saucepan until tender; drain well. Sauté green pepper and onion in margarine in skillet until tender. Add to potatoes. Add parsley, salt, pepper and enough paprika to color. Serve immediately or microwave to reheat. Yield: 4 servings.

Approx Per Serving: Cal 189; Prot 4 g; Carbo 38 g; Fiber 5 g;
T Fat 3 g; Chol 0 mg; Sod 43 mg.

Dietary Exchanges: Vegetable 1/2; Bread/Starch 2; Fat 1/2

HASHED BROWN POTATOES

2 large potatoes
2 tablespoons finely chopped
  onion
1 clove of garlic, minced

1/2 teaspoon thyme
Salt and pepper to taste

Cook potatoes in water to cover in saucepan until tender; drain and cool slightly. Peel and shred potatoes. Combine with onion, garlic, thyme, salt and pepper in bowl; mix lightly. Preheat 10-inch skillet sprayed with nonstick spray over medium heat. Add potato mixture. Cook for 6 to 7 minutes or until bottom is brown. Invert onto plate. Return to skillet browned side up. Cook for 6 to 7 minutes or until bottom is brown. Cut into wedges. Yield: 4 servings.

Approx Per Serving: Cal 74; Prot 2 g; Carbo 17 g; Fiber 2 g;
    T Fat <1 g; Chol 0 mg; Sod 4 mg.

Dietary Exchanges: Bread/Starch 1

NACHO POTATO WEDGES

3 potatoes, baked in skins
1 tablespoon melted
  margarine
Pepper to taste
Chili powder to taste

3 ounces Monterey Jack
  cheese, shredded
3 tablespoons thinly sliced
  scallions

Cool potatoes completely. Cut into wedges lengthwise. Place cut side up in single layer on baking sheet. Brush with melted margarine; sprinkle with pepper. Broil for 10 minutes or until light brown. Sprinkle with chili powder, cheese and scallions. Broil for 1 to 2 minutes or until cheese is melted. Yield: 6 servings.

Approx Per Serving: Cal 132; Prot 6 g; Carbo 18 g; Fiber 2 g;
    T Fat 5 g; Chol 8 mg; Sod 87 mg.

Dietary Exchanges: Bread/Starch 1; Meat 1/2; Fat 1/2

SCALLOPED POTATOES

3 tablespoons corn oil
  margarine
1/4 cup flour
1 teaspoon salt
1/8 teaspoon pepper

3 cups skim milk
6 medium potatoes, peeled,
  thinly sliced
2 tablespoons chopped onion

Blend margarine, flour, salt and pepper in saucepan. Add milk gradually. Cook until thickened, stirring constantly. Layer potatoes, onion and sauce 1/2 at a time in greased 2-quart baking dish. Bake, covered, at 350 degrees for 1 hour. Bake, uncovered, for 30 minutes longer. Yield: 8 servings.

Approx Per Serving: Cal 175; Prot 5 g; Carbo 28 g; Fiber 1 g;
  T Fat 5 g; Chol 2 mg; Sod 346 mg.

Dietary Exchanges: Milk 1/2; Bread/Starch 1 1/2; Fat 1

RATATOUILLE

1 29-ounce can tomatoes,
   chopped
1 15-ounce can tomatoes,
   chopped
1 large onion, chopped
1/2 green bell pepper, chopped

1 eggplant, peeled, cubed
3 medium zucchini, cubed
1 teaspoon (or more) oregano
Salt and pepper to taste
2 tablespoons olive oil

Bring undrained tomatoes to a boil in heavy saucepan. Add onion and green pepper. Cook until onion is transparent. Add eggplant, zucchini, oregano, salt and pepper; reduce heat. Simmer for 1 hour. Add olive oil. Cook for 10 minutes longer. Serve hot or cold. Yield: 10 servings.

Approx Per Serving: Cal 71; Prot 2 g; Carbo 10 g; Fiber 3 g;
  T Fat 3 g; Chol 0 mg; Sod 205 mg.

Dietary Exchanges: Vegetable 2; Fat 1/2

STIR-FRIED SNOW PEAS

1/4 cup chicken broth
1 teaspoon cornstarch
1 or 2 cloves of garlic, minced
1 8-ounce can sliced
    bamboo shoots, drained

2 cups fresh snow peas
1 8-ounce can sliced water
    chestnuts, drained
2 teaspoons reduced-sodium
    soy sauce

Blend chicken broth and cornstarch in small bowl; set aside. Preheat skillet sprayed with nonstick cooking spray over low heat. Add garlic. Sauté until light brown. Add bamboo shoots, snow peas, water chestnuts and soy sauce. Increase heat. Stir-fry over high heat for 1 minute; reduce heat to medium. Stir in chicken broth mixture. Cook until thickened, stirring constantly. Yield: 4 servings.

Approx Per Serving: Cal 78; Prot 4 g; Carbo 16 g; Fiber 5 g;
    T Fat 1 g; Chol <1 mg; Sod 189 mg.

Dietary Exchanges: Vegetable 1 1/2; Bread/Starch 1/2

SNOW PEAS AND TOMATOES

1/4 cup chopped onion
1 tablespoon corn oil
    margarine
1 pound fresh snow peas,
    trimmed
1 tablespoon reduced-
    sodium soy sauce

1 teaspoon fresh oregano or
    1/2 teaspoon dried oregano
3 medium tomatoes, cut into
    wedges

Sauté onion in margarine in skillet over medium heat. Add snow peas, soy sauce and oregano. Stir-fry for 3 minutes or until tender-crisp. Add tomatoes. Cook, covered, for 1 minute. Yield: 6 servings.

Approx Per Serving: Cal 65; Prot 3 g; Carbo 9 g; Fiber 5 g;
    T Fat 2 g; Chol 0 mg; Sod 159 mg.

Dietary Exchanges: Vegetable 1/2; Bread/Starch 1/2; Fat 1/2

MICROWAVE ACORN SQUASH WITH CRANBERRIES

1 large acorn squash
1 tablespoon water
1/2 cup cranberries
2 tablespoons thawed frozen
  apple juice concentrate
1 tablespoon water

1 tablespoon finely chopped
  onion
2 teaspoons sugar
1 tablespoon thawed frozen
  apple juice concentrate
Salt and pepper to taste

Cut squash into halves, discarding seed. Place cut side down in 10-inch glass pie plate. Add 1 tablespoon water. Microwave, loosely covered with waxed paper, on High for 8 to 10 minutes or until tender, rotating dish once. Let stand, covered, for several minutes. Combine cranberries, 2 tablespoons apple juice concentrate, 1 tablespoon water, onion and sugar in 4-cup glass measure. Microwave for 4 to 5 minutes or until thickened, stirring once. Drain squash and cut each half lengthwise into halves. Place cut side up in glass plate. Brush with 1 tablespoon apple juice concentrate. Sprinkle with salt and pepper. Top with cranberry mixture. Microwave on High for 30 seconds to 1 minute or until heated through. Yield: 4 servings.

Approx Per Serving: Cal 149; Prot 2 g; Carbo 38 g; Fiber 5 g;
    T Fat <1 g; Chol 0 mg; Sod 12 mg.

Dietary Exchanges: Bread/Starch 2 1/2

MICROWAVE SQUASH WITH BASIL

1 tablespoon julienne fresh
  basil leaves
2 teaspoons grated lemon rind
1/4 teaspoon minced garlic
Salt and freshly ground
  pepper to taste

8 ounces zucchini, sliced 1/2
  inch thick
8 ounces yellow squash,
  sliced 1/2 inch thick
1 tablespoon water

Mix basil, lemon rind, garlic, salt and pepper in small bowl; set aside. Combine zucchini, yellow squash and water in 2 or 3-quart glass dish with glass lid. Microwave, covered, on High for 3 minutes. Shake dish to rearrange squash. Microwave for 1 to 2 minutes or until tender-crisp. Let stand, covered, for 2 minutes. Add basil mixture; toss to mix well. Yield: 4 servings.

Approx Per Serving: Cal 18; Prot 1 g; Carbo 4 g; Fiber 2 g,
    T Fat <1 g; Chol 0 mg; Sod 3 mg.

Dietary Exchanges: Vegetable 1

MICROWAVE SPAGHETTI SQUASH WITH VEGETABLES

1 spaghetti squash
1 tablespoon olive oil
1 clove of garlic
1/2 teaspoon salt
2 cups chopped fresh tomatoes
4 large fresh basil leaves, cut
　into strips
Salt and freshly ground
　pepper to taste

1 1/2 cups broccoli flowerets
1 large carrot, thinly sliced
　on the diagonal
2 tablespoons water
2 ounces snow peas,
　trimmed, thinly sliced on
　the diagonal
2 tablespoons Parmesan
　cheese

Pierce squash through to center 6 times with sharp knife. Microwave on High for 12 minutes, turning after 6 minutes. Let stand, covered with towel, for 10 minutes. Mash garlic with 1/2 teaspoon salt in small bowl. Combine with tomatoes in 2 or 3-quart glass dish. Microwave on High for 3 minutes or until tomatoes are tender, stirring once. Stir in basil, salt and pepper. Combine broccoli, carrot and water in 10-inch glass pie plate. Microwave, loosely covered with waxed paper, on High for 2 minutes. Add snow peas. Microwave for 1 minute or until vegetables are tender. Let stand, covered, for 5 minutes. Cut squash into halves lengthwise. Discard seed and center pith. Pull squash from shell with fork, adding to tomato mixture. Drain vegetables. Add to squash mixture; toss with fork. Sprinkle with cheese. Serve immediately. Yield: 4 servings.

Approx Per Serving: Cal 102; Prot 4 g; Carbo 13 g; Fiber 4 g;
　T Fat 5 g; Chol 2 mg; Sod 338 mg.

Dietary Exchanges: Vegetable 1; Bread/Starch 1/2; Meat 1/2; Fat 1/2

SUMMER SQUASH CASSEROLE

4 cups sliced yellow squash
1 onion, thinly sliced
2 tomatoes, thinly sliced
Salt and pepper to taste

1/2 cup shredded mozzarella
　cheese
1/2 cup shredded Cheddar
　cheese

Layer squash, onion and tomatoes in baking dish sprayed with nonstick cooking spray. Season with salt and pepper. Bake at 350 degrees for 30 to 40 minutes or until tender. Top with cheeses. Bake for 5 minutes longer. Yield: 6 servings.

Approx Per Serving: Cal 106; Prot 6 g; Carbo 9 g; Fiber 3 g;
　T Fat 6 g; Chol 17 mg; Sod 100 mg.

Dietary Exchanges: Vegetable 1 1/2; Meat 1/2; Fat 1/2

SPINACH WILT

1 bunch fresh spinach
1 teaspoon minced garlic

1 tablespoon olive oil

Wash spinach and pat very dry. Sauté garlic in olive oil in heavy saucepan; remove from heat. Let stand for several minutes. Add spinach. Cook over medium heat until spinach begins to steam. Stir and cover spinach. Cook for 10 minutes, stirring once after 5 minutes. Serve immediately. Yield: 2 servings.

Approx Per Serving: Cal 86; Prot 3 g; Carbo 4 g; Fiber 4 g;
T Fat 7 g; Chol 0 mg; Sod 89 mg.

Dietary Exchanges: Vegetable 1; Fat 1½

CANDIED SWEET POTATOES

3 medium sweet potatoes
1½ teaspoons cornstarch
½ cup unsweetened pineapple juice

1 teaspoon sugar
⅛ teaspoon maple extract
1½ tablespoons margarine

Cook potatoes in water to cover in saucepan for 20 minutes or until nearly tender. Peel and slice lengthwise ½ inch thick. Arrange in baking dish. Blend cornstarch, pineapple juice, sugar and maple extract in small saucepan. Add margarine. Cook until thickened, stirring constantly. Spoon over sweet potatoes. Bake at 375 degrees until glazed. May substitute fructose for sugar if preferred. Yield: 6 servings.

Approx Per Serving: Cal 101; Prot 1 g; Carbo 18 g; Fiber 1 g;
T Fat 3 g; Chol 0 mg; Sod 39 mg.

Dietary Exchanges: Bread/Starch 1; Fat ½

☎ Make a tasty **Yogurt Spread** for vegetables, bread or baked potatoes by draining 8 ounces plain nonfat yogurt in a funnel or sieve lined with cheesecloth for 2 to 4 hours. Stir in one ½-ounce package of Butter Buds for **Yogurt-Butter Spread**.

GINGERED SWEET POTATOES

1 29-ounce can sweet
   potatoes
1 16-ounce can apricots in
   light syrup, drained

1 8-ounce can pineapple
   tidbits, drained
4 pieces candied ginger,
   sliced

Cut sweet potatoes into 1/2-inch slices. Cut apricots into quarters. Drain pineapple, reserving juice. Alternate layers of sweet potatoes, apricots and pineapple in 1 1/2-quart baking dish, sprinkling layers with ginger. Pour reserved juice over layers. Bake, covered, at 350 degrees for 40 minutes. Yield: 8 servings.

Approx Per Serving: Cal 160; Prot 2 g; Carbo 38 g; Fiber 3 g;
    T Fat <1 g; Chol 0 mg; Sod 80 mg.

Dietary Exchanges: Fruit 1; Bread/Starch 1 1/2

SWEET POTATO AND APPLE CASSEROLE

3 large Granny Smith apples,
   peeled, thinly sliced
1 tablespoon lemon juice
1 1/2 pounds sweet potatoes

1/4 cup apple juice
1 tablespoon melted
   margarine

Toss apples with lemon juice in bowl. Peel sweet potatoes; cut into halves lengthwise and slice thinly. Reserve several slices sweet potato. Alternate layers of remaining sweet potatoes and apples in 1 1/2-quart baking dish. Arrange reserved sweet potato slices in overlapping circle on top of layers. Drizzle with apple juice and margarine. Bake, covered, at 350 degrees for 1 hour. Bake, uncovered, for 15 minutes longer or until top is brown. Yield: 6 servings.

Approx Per Serving: Cal 176; Prot 2 g; Carbo 39 g; Fiber 3 g;
    T Fat 2 g; Chol 0 mg; Sod 34 mg.

Dietary Exchanges: Fruit 1; Bread/Starch 2; Fat 1/2

TOMATO AND CORN BAKE

4 small tomatoes
Salt to taste
1 16-ounce can whole kernel
   corn, drained

1/2 cup shredded Swiss
   cheese
1 tablespoon sliced green
   onions

Cut tomatoes into halves crosswise. Remove and discard pulp, reserving shells. Sprinkle inside of tomato shells with salt. Invert on paper towel to drain. Combine corn, cheese and green onions in bowl; mix well. Spoon into tomato shells; place in 9x13-inch baking dish. Bake at 350 degrees for 20 to 25 minutes or until heated through. Yield: 8 servings.

Approx Per Serving: Cal 82; Prot 4 g; Carbo 13 g; Fiber 2 g;
   T Fat 2 g; Chol 6 mg; Sod 265 mg.

Dietary Exchanges: Vegetable 1/2; Bread/Starch 1/2; Meat 1/2; Fat 1/2

GREEK ZUCCHINI

8 small zucchini
2/3 cup water
1 medium onion, chopped
1 clove of garlic, chopped

1 tablespoon margarine
4 tomatoes, peeled, chopped
Salt and pepper to taste

Score zucchini lengthwise with fork. Cook in water in saucepan for 6 minutes or until tender. Sauté onion and garlic in margarine in medium skillet over medium heat. Add tomatoes. Cook until tender. Season with salt and pepper. Drain zucchini. Arrange zucchini on serving plate. Spoon tomato sauce over top. May top with favorite cheese. Yield: 8 servings.

Approx Per Serving: Cal 51; Prot 2 g; Carbo 8 g; Fiber 3 g;
   T Fat 2 g; Chol 0 mg; Sod 25 mg.

Dietary Exchanges: Vegetable 1 1/2; Fat 1/2

BROWN RICE PILAF

1/2 cup uncooked brown rice
1/3 cup chopped onion
1/3 cup sliced fresh
  mushrooms

1/4 teaspoon fresh thyme
Pepper to taste
11/4 cups chicken broth
1/2 cup thinly sliced celery

Combine rice, onion, mushrooms, thyme and pepper in 1-quart baking dish. Stir in broth. Bake, covered, at 350 degrees for 1 hour. Stir in celery. Bake, covered, for 10 to 15 minutes or until celery is tender and liquid is absorbed. Yield: 4 servings.

Approx Per Serving: Cal 104; Prot 4 g; Carbo 20 g; Fiber 1 g;
  T Fat 1 g; Chol <1 mg; Sod 259 mg.

Dietary Exchanges: Vegetable 1/2; Bread/Starch 11/2; Meat 1/2

RICE SUPREME

1 cup thinly sliced carrots
1 tablespoon margarine
11/4 cups water
3/4 cup apple juice
2 tablespoons lemon juice
2 tablespoons light brown
  sugar

Salt to taste
1 cup uncooked rice
1/2 cup raisins
1/2 teaspoon cinnamon
2 cups sliced unpeeled apples
1/2 cup sliced green onions

Sauté carrots in margarine in large skillet over low heat for 5 minutes or until tender-crisp. Add water, apple juice, lemon juice, brown sugar and salt; mix well. Bring to a boil over medium heat. Stir in rice, raisins and cinnamon; reduce heat. Simmer, covered, for 15 minutes or until rice is tender. Stir in apples and green onions. Cook until heated through. Garnish with sesame seed.
Yield: 6 servings.

Approx Per Serving: Cal 233; Prot 3 g; Carbo 51 g; Fiber 3 g;
  T Fat 2 g; Chol 0 mg; Sod 35 mg.

Dietary Exchanges: Vegetable 1/2; Fruit 11/2; Bread/Starch 11/2; Fat 1/2

Breads

BREADS

QUICK LOW-CHOLESTEROL BISCUITS

2 cups self-rising flour   **¼ cup corn oil**
⅔ cup buttermilk

    Combine flour, buttermilk and oil in medium bowl; stir just until moistened. Knead several times on floured surface. Roll ½ inch thick. Cut with 2-inch biscuit cutter. Place on baking sheet. Bake at 425 degrees for 10 to 12 minutes or until golden brown. Yield: 12 servings.

Approx Per Serving: Cal 119; Prot 2 g; Carbo 16 g; Fiber 1 g;
    T Fat 5 g; Chol <1 mg; Sod 239 mg.

Dietary Exchanges: Bread/Starch 1; Fat 1

WHOLE WHEAT BUTTERMILK BISCUITS

½ cup all-purpose flour   **¼ teaspoon salt**
½ cup whole wheat flour   **3 tablespoons corn oil**
1½ teaspoons baking powder   **margarine**
1 teaspoon sugar   **7 tablespoons buttermilk**
¼ teaspoon soda

    Combine flours, baking powder, sugar, soda and salt in bowl; mix well. Cut in margarine until crumbly. Stir in buttermilk. Knead 4 or 5 times on lightly floured surface. Roll ½ inch thick. Cut with 2-inch biscuit cutter. Place on baking sheet sprayed with nonstick cooking spray. Bake at 400 degrees for 10 minutes or until light brown. Yield: 10 servings.

Approx Per Serving: Cal 80; Prot 2 g; Carbo 10 g; Fiber <1 g;
    T Fat 4 g; Chol <1 mg; Sod 172 mg.

Dietary Exchanges: Bread/Starch ½; Fat ½

☎ Use low-fat buttermilk and cut biscuits with 1½-inch cutter to reduce calories in each serving.

SESAME CRACKERS

1 1/3 cups whole wheat flour
1 cup all-purpose flour
1/4 cup soy flour
1/4 cup sesame seed
1/3 cup wheat germ

1/4 cup packed brown sugar
1 teaspoon salt
1/2 cup canola oil
1 cup cold water

Combine flours, sesame seed, wheat germ, brown sugar and salt in bowl; mix well. Sprinkle oil and water over dry ingredients; mix well. Shape into ball. Knead on floured surface until smooth. Divide into 4 portions. Roll each portion into thin circle on floured surface. Cut into 1-inch crackers. Place on baking sheet sprayed with nonstick cooking spray; prick with fork. Bake at 325 degrees until light brown. Yield: 48 servings.

Approx Per Serving: Cal 54; Prot 1 g; Carbo 6 g; Fiber 1 g;
    T Fat 3 g; Chol 0 mg; Sod 41 mg.

Dietary Exchanges: Bread/Starch 1/2; Fat 1/2

BROCCOLI CORN BREAD

1 cup chopped onion
1 10-ounce package frozen
    chopped broccoli, thawed
4 eggs, beaten
1/2 cup melted margarine

3/4 cup cottage cheese
1 teaspoon salt
1 7-ounce package corn
    muffin mix

Combine onion, broccoli, eggs, margarine, cottage cheese and salt in bowl; mix well. Add muffin mix; stir just until moistened. Spoon into greased 9x13-inch baking dish. Bake at 400 degrees for 20 minutes or until golden brown. Yield: 12 servings.

Approx Per Serving: Cal 153; Prot 5 g; Carbo 9 g; Fiber 1 g;
    T Fat 11 g; Chol 93 mg; Sod 413 mg.

Dietary Exchanges: Vegetable 1/2; Bread/Starch 1/2; Meat 1; Fat 2

☎ Use 1 cup egg substitute for eggs and low-fat cottage cheese to reduce calories in fat and cholesterol in **Broccoli Corn Bread**.

MEXICAN CORN BREAD

1 cup self-rising cornmeal
1/2 teaspoon cayenne pepper
1/2 cup chopped green bell
  pepper
1/2 cup shredded low-fat
  Cheddar cheese
1/2 cup chopped onion
1 cup skim milk
2 eggs, beaten
1 8½-ounce can cream-style
  corn

Combine cornmeal and cayenne pepper in bowl. Add green pepper, cheese, onion, milk, eggs and corn; mix well. Spoon into 8x8-inch baking dish sprayed with nonstick cooking spray. Bake at 450 degrees for 25 minutes or until golden brown. Cut into 2-inch squares. Yield: 16 servings.

Approx Per Serving: Cal 68; Prot 3 g; Carbo 10 g; Fiber <1 g;
    T Fat 2 g; Chol 36 mg; Sod 63 mg.

Dietary Exchanges: Bread/Starch 1/2; Meat 1/2

SUGARLESS BANANA BREAD

2 eggs, beaten
1/2 cup honey
1/2 cup oil
3 bananas, mashed
2 cups flour
1 teaspoon soda
1/2 cup raisins
1 cup chopped walnuts

Combine eggs, honey and oil in bowl; mix well. Add bananas; mix well. Stir in mixture of flour and soda just until moistened. Fold in raisins and walnuts. Pour into greased 5x9-inch loaf pan. Bake at 350 degrees for 1 hour or until loaf tests done. Yield: 14 servings.

Approx Per Serving: Cal 255; Prot 5 g; Carbo 34 g; Fiber 2 g;
    T Fat 12 g; Chol 39 mg; Sod 70 mg.

Dietary Exchanges: Fruit 1/2; Bread/Starch 1; Meat 1/2; Fat 2½

☎ Although most oils have similar calorie counts, some have less saturated fat than others. Canola oil is considered to be one of the healthiest and can be substituted for any vegetable oil.

BLESS-YOUR-HEART BREAD

2 envelopes dry yeast
1/2 cup warm water
1/4 cup margarine
2 cups skim milk, scalded
1/2 cup molasses
1/4 cup honey
2 tablespoons brown sugar

1 cup whole wheat flour
1 cup oats
1/4 cup bran cereal
1/3 cup rye flour
4 to 5 cups unbleached flour
2 teaspoons salt
1 teaspoon ginger

Dissolve yeast in warm water. Combine margarine and hot milk in bowl; stir until margarine melts. Add molasses, honey and brown sugar. Let stand until lukewarm. Add yeast; mix well. Combine whole wheat flour, oats, cereal and rye flour in bowl; mix well. Add milk mixture gradually, mixing well after each addition. Add enough unbleached flour to make medium dough. Knead on floured surface for 4 to 5 minutes. Place in greased bowl, turning to coat surface. Let rise, covered with damp cloth, until doubled in bulk. Shape into 2 loaves; place in 2 greased 5x9-inch loaf pans. Let rise for 1 to 1 1/2 hours or until doubled in bulk. Bake at 325 degrees for 40 minutes or until loaves test done. Yield: 28 servings.

Approx Per Serving: Cal 161; Prot 4 g; Carbo 31 g; Fiber 2 g;
    T Fat 2 g; Chol <1 mg; Sod 182 mg.

Dietary Exchanges: Bread/Starch 1 1/2; Fat 1/2

ENGLISH MUFFIN LOAVES

2 cups warm milk
1/2 cup warm water
2 envelopes dry yeast
1/2 teaspoon sugar
5 cups flour

3/4 cup untoasted wheat germ
1 tablespoon sugar
1 teaspoon salt
1/4 teaspoon soda
1/4 cup cornmeal

Combine first 4 ingredients in mixer bowl. Let stand until yeast dissolves. Add flour, wheat germ, 1 tablespoon sugar, salt and soda; mix well. Mixture will be thick. Grease bottoms and sides of two 1-pound coffee cans. Sprinkle with cornmeal. Spoon batter into cans. Let rise, covered, for 1 hour or until dough reaches tops of cans. Bake at 400 degrees for 25 to 30 minutes or until loaves test done. Remove to wire rack to cool. Slice and serve toasted. Yield: 20 servings.

Approx Per Serving: Cal 155; Prot 6 g; Carbo 29 g; Fiber 1 g;
    T Fat 2 g; Chol 3 mg; Sod 121 mg.

Dietary Exchanges: Bread/Starch 2; Fat 1/2

HONEY-OAT BREAD

1²/₃ cups bread flour
1 cup oats
¹/₂ cup unprocessed oat bran
1¹/₂ teaspoons salt
3 envelopes dry yeast
1³/₄ cups water
¹/₂ cup honey

¹/₂ cup oil
¹/₂ cup egg substitute
2¹/₂ cups whole wheat flour
³/₄ cup bread flour
1 egg white
1 tablespoon water

Combine 1²/₃ cups bread flour, oats, oat bran, salt and yeast in bowl; mix well. Combine water, honey and oil in saucepan. Heat to 120 to 130 degrees on candy thermometer. Add with egg substitute to flour mixture. Beat at low speed until blended. Beat at medium speed for 3 minutes. Stir in whole wheat flour gradually. Add ¹/₄ cup bread flour. Knead for 10 minutes or until smooth and elastic, adding enough remaining ¹/₂ cup bread flour 1 tablespoon at a time to make dough easy to handle. Place in bowl sprayed with nonstick cooking spray, turning to coat surface. Let rise, covered, in warm place for 1 hour or until doubled in bulk. Punch dough down. Let rest for 15 minutes. Shape into 2 loaves. Place each in 5x9-inch loaf pan coated with nonstick cooking spray. Let rise, covered, for 15 minutes or until doubled in bulk. Brush with mixture of egg white and 1 tablespoon water. Bake at 375 degrees for 35 to 40 minutes or until loaves test done. Cover with foil during last 10 minutes of baking time to prevent overbrowning if necessary. Remove loaves to wire rack to cool. Cut into ¹/₂-inch slices. Yield: 36 servings.

Approx Per Serving: Cal 116; Prot 3 g; Carbo 19 g; Fiber 2 g;
    T Fat 4 g; Chol <1 mg; Sod 90 mg.

Dietary Exchanges: Bread/Starch 1; Fat ¹/₂

☎ Egg whites or egg substitute in the amount of ¹/₄ cup per egg may be substituted for eggs in most breads to lower calories, fat and cholesterol.

CRACKED WHEAT BREAD

3/4 cup cracked wheat
2 1/4 cups all-purpose flour
2 envelopes dry yeast
1/4 cup packed brown sugar
4 teaspoons salt

2 1/2 cups warm wate
2 tablespoons safflo\
2 cups whole wheat fl\
1 3/4 to 2 3/4 cups all-pur| ⌐se
    flour

Combine cracked wheat and enough water to cover in saucepan. Cook using package directions for 30 minutes. Drain; set aside. Combine 2 1/4 cups all-purpose flour, yeast, brown sugar and salt in mixer bowl; mix well. Add warm water and oil. Beat at low speed until moistened. Beat at medium speed for 3 minutes. Add whole wheat flour and cracked wheat gradually, mixing well after each addition. Add enough remaining all-purpose flour to form stiff dough. Knead on floured surface for 5 to 8 minutes or until smooth and elastic. Place in greased bowl, turning to coat surface. Let rise, covered, in warm place for 1 hour or until doubled in bulk. Shape into 2 loaves. Sprinkle with additional uncooked cracked wheat. Place on greased baking sheets. Let rise, covered, for 30 minutes or until doubled in bulk. Bake at 375 degrees for 25 to 30 minutes or until golden brown. Remove to wire rack to cool. Yield: 32 servings.

Approx Per Serving: Cal 125; Prot 4 g; Carbo 25 g; Fiber 2 g;
    T Fat 1 g; Chol 0 mg; Sod 246 mg.

Dietary Exchanges: Bread/Starch 1 1/2

APPLE AND OAT BRAN MUFFINS

1 1/4 cups whole wheat flour
1 cup oat bran
1/3 cup packed brown sugar
1/4 teaspoon soda
2 1/2 teaspoons baking powder
1/4 teaspoon salt

1/4 teaspoon nutmeg
1/4 teaspoon cinnamon
1 cup buttermilk
2 egg whites
2 tablespoons oil
3/4 cup shredded peeled apple

Combine first 8 ingredients in bowl; stir to mix well. Combine buttermilk, egg whites and oil in bowl; mix well. Add to dry ingredients. Stir just until moistened. Fold in apple. Store, tightly covered, in refrigerator for up to 5 days. Fill muffin cups sprayed with nonstick cooking spray with 1/4 cup batter. Bake at 375 degrees for 18 to 20 minutes or until brown. Yield: 12 servings.

Approx Per Serving: Cal 119; Prot 4 g; Carbo 22 g; Fiber 3 g;
    T Fat 3 g; Chol 1 mg; Sod 162 mg.

Dietary Exchanges: Bread/Starch 1; Fat 1/2

WHOLE WHEAT APPLE MUFFINS

1 cup oats
1 cup whole wheat pastry
 flour
1 teaspoon baking powder
1/2 teaspoon soda
1/4 teaspoon salt

1/4 teaspoon cinnamon
1/4 teaspoon nutmeg
1 cup chopped apples
1 cup plain yogurt
1/4 cup honey
2 tablespoons oil

Combine oats, whole wheat pastry flour, baking powder, soda, salt and spices in bowl; stir to mix well. Combine apples, yogurt, honey and oil in bowl; mix well. Add to dry ingredients. Stir just until moistened. Fill greased muffin cups 3/4 full. Bake at 400 degrees for 15 to 20 minutes or until muffins test done. Yield: 12 servings.

Approx Per Serving: Cal 119; Prot 3 g; Carbo 20 g; Fiber 2 g;
 T Fat 3 g; Chol 1 mg; Sod 117 mg.

Dietary Exchanges: Bread/Starch 1; Fat 1/2

BANANA OAT MUFFINS

2 tablespoons oat bran
1 ripe banana, mashed
12/3 cups skim milk
1 teaspoon safflower oil
1/3 cup honey
1 teaspoon vanilla extract

1/2 cup chopped peeled apple
1/4 cup raisins
21/2 cups oat bran
1 tablespoon baking powder
3/4 teaspoon soda
1 teaspoon cinnamon

Grease muffin pans. Sprinkle with 2 tablespoons oat bran. Combine banana, milk, oil, honey, vanilla, apple and raisins in bowl; mix well. Combine 21/2 cups oat bran, baking powder, soda and cinnamon in bowl; mix well. Add to banana mixture. Stir just until moistened. Fill prepared muffin cups 2/3 full. Bake at 400 degrees for 25 minutes or until light brown. Cool in pan for 5 minutes. Yield: 12 servings.

Approx Per Serving: Cal 111; Prot 5 g; Carbo 28 g; Fiber 4 g;
 T Fat 1 g; Chol 1 mg; Sod 159 mg.

Dietary Exchanges: Fruit 1/2; Bread/Starch 1

☎ Line muffin cups with paper liners to eliminate need for greasing muffin cups and to reduce calories and fat.

WHOLE WHEAT BANANA BRAN MUFFINS

1¼ cups whole wheat flour
⅓ cup sugar
1 tablespoon baking powder
1½ cups whole bran cereal

¾ cup skim milk
1 cup mashed ripe bananas
1 egg
¼ cup safflower oil

Combine whole wheat flour, sugar and baking powder in bowl; stir to mix well. Combine bran cereal, milk and bananas in bowl; mix well. Let stand for 5 minutes or until cereal is softened. Add egg and oil; mix well. Stir in flour mixture just until moistened. Spoon into paper-lined muffin cups. Bake at 400 degrees for 25 minutes. Yield: 18 servings.

Approx Per Serving: Cal 102; Prot 2 g; Carbo 16 g; Fiber 2 g;
T Fat 4 g; Chol 15 mg; Sod 104 mg.

Dietary Exchanges: Bread/Starch ½; Fat ½

BLUEBERRY-OAT BRAN MUFFINS

2¼ cups oat bran
¼ cup packed brown sugar
1 tablespoon baking powder
½ teaspoon salt
⅓ cup nonfat dry milk
¾ cup water

2 tablespoons egg substitute
1 egg white, beaten
¼ cup honey
1 tablespoon olive oil
1½ cups fresh blueberries

Combine oat bran, brown sugar, baking powder and salt in bowl; stir to mix well. Dissolve milk powder in ¾ cup water in bowl. Add egg substitute, honey, olive oil and egg white. Add to dry ingredients; stir just until moistened. Fold in blueberries. Fill paper-lined muffin cups ⅔ full. Bake at 425 degrees for 15 minutes. Serve warm with Yogurt-Butter Spread (page 137) or as dessert with fresh fruit and frozen yogurt. Store, covered, in refrigerator and reheat in microwave on High for 12 seconds per muffin. Yield: 12 servings.

Approx Per Serving: Cal 111; Prot 5 g; Carbo 26 g; Fiber 3 g;
T Fat 2 g; Chol <1 mg; Sod 192 mg.

Dietary Exchanges: Bread/Starch 1; Fat ½

☎ Serve muffins with jam instead of butter to reduce calories and fat.

WHOLE WHEAT CORN MUFFINS

1/4 cup whole wheat flour
1/4 cup white cornmeal
2 teaspoons sugar
1 teaspoon baking powder

1/8 teaspoon salt
1/4 cup skim milk
1 egg white
1 tablespoon oil

Combine whole wheat flour, cornmeal, sugar, baking powder and salt in bowl; stir to mix well. Add milk, egg white and oil; stir just until moistened. Fill muffin cups sprayed with nonstick cooking spray 2/3 full. Bake at 425 degrees for 20 minutes or until light brown. Yield: 4 servings.

Approx Per Serving: Cal 105; Prot 3 g; Carbo 15 g; Fiber 1 g;
T Fat 4 g; Chol <1 mg; Sod 167 mg.

Dietary Exchanges: Bread/Starch 1; Fat 1/2

OAT BRAN MUFFINS

2 1/4 cups unprocessed oat
bran
1/4 cup packed brown sugar
1 teaspoon baking powder
1/4 teaspoon salt

3/4 cup skim milk
1/2 cup egg substitute
1/4 cup honey
2 teaspoons oil

Combine oat bran, brown sugar, baking powder and salt in bowl; stir to mix well. Make well in center. Combine milk, egg substitute, honey and oil in bowl; mix well. Add to dry ingredients; stir just until moistened. Fill muffin cups sprayed with nonstick cooking spray 3/4 full. Bake at 425 degrees for 15 minutes. Yield: 12 servings.

Approx Per Serving: Cal 100; Prot 5 g; Carbo 23 g; Fiber 3 g;
T Fat 2 g; Chol <1 mg; Sod 101 mg.

Dietary Exchanges: Bread/Starch 1; Fat 1/2

Raisin-Oat Bran Muffins: Add 1/3 cup raisins to batter. Adds 13 calories per muffin.

Banana-Oat Bran Muffins: Add 1/2 cup mashed ripe banana to batter. Adds 8 calories per muffin.

Blueberry-Oat Bran Muffins: Add 1/2 cup fresh or thawed, frozen blueberries to batter. Adds 4 calories per muffin.

Apple-Cinnamon-Oat Bran Muffins: Add 1/2 cup minced apple and 1 teaspoon cinnamon to batter. Adds 3 calories per muffin.

OATMEAL MUFFINS

1 cup oats
1 cup skim milk buttermilk
1 teaspoon soda
1/2 cup oil

1 egg, beaten
1 teaspoon salt
1/2 cup packed brown sugar

Combine oats and buttermilk in bowl; mix well. Let stand for 20 minutes, Add soda, oil and egg; mix well. Add salt and brown sugar; mix well. Spoon into greased muffin cups. Bake at 425 degrees for 15 to 20 minutes or until muffins test done. Yield: 12 servings.

Approx Per Serving: Cal 155; Prot 2 g; Carbo 14 g; Fiber <1 g;
    T Fat 10 g; Chol 24 mg; Sod 262 mg.

Dietary Exchanges: Bread/Starch 1/2; Fat 2

CORN BREAD PANCAKES

1 1/2 cups self-rising cornmeal
1/8 teaspoon salt
1/2 cup buttermilk
2 tablespoons egg substitute

1/2 teaspoon to 1 tablespoon
    olive oil
1 tablespoon (about) water

Combine cornmeal, salt, buttermilk, egg substitute and olive oil in bowl; mix well. Add enough water to make of desired consistency. Spoon onto hot griddle sprayed with nonstick cooking spray. Bake until pancakes are firm and edges start to brown. Turn pancakes over. Bake until golden brown on bottom. Yield: 12 pancakes.

Approx Per Pancake: Cal 104; Prot 3 g; Carbo 21 g; Fiber 0 g;
    T Fat 1 g; Chol <1 mg; Sod 117 mg.

Dietary Exchanges: Bread/Starch 1 1/2

☎ Make delicious breakfast or dessert **Banana Pancakes** by mixing 2 cups baking mix with 2 eggs, 1 cup skim milk and 1/2 cup plain yogurt. Ladle batter onto hot griddle, add banana slices and cover with batter. Bake as usual and serve with syrup, flavored yogurt or fruit.

HEALTHY PANCAKE MIX

3/4 cup all-purpose flour
1/4 cup whole wheat flour
1/2 cup ground oats
1/4 cup dry buttermilk powder
2 tablespoons sugar
1 1/2 teaspoons baking powder

1/2 teaspoon soda
1/4 teaspoon salt
1 cup water
3 tablespoons oil
2 eggs, slightly beaten

Combine all-purpose flour, whole wheat flour, oats, buttermilk powder, sugar, baking powder, soda and salt in bowl; mix well. Store mix in airtight container until ready to use. To prepare pancakes: Combine water, oil and eggs in bowl; mix well. Add pancake mix; mix well. Ladle 1/4 cup batter at a time onto hot greased griddle. Bake for 3 to 4 minutes or until golden brown, turning once. May substitute crushed oat bran cereal for ground oats. Yield: 12 pancakes.

Approx Per Pancake: Cal 114; Prot 4 g; Carbo 14 g; Fiber 1 g;
     T Fat 5 g; Chol 47 mg; Sod 142 mg.

Dietary Exchanges: Bread/Starch 1/2; Fat 1

WHOLE WHEAT PITA BREAD

1 envelope dry yeast
3 cups whole wheat flour
1 teaspoon salt
1 1/2 teaspoons sugar

2 1/2 cups lukewarm water
2 tablespoons oil
3 cups whole wheat flour

Combine yeast, 3 cups flour, salt and sugar in mixer bowl. Add water and oil. Beat at medium speed for 3 minutes. Stir in enough remaining 3 cups flour to make stiff dough. Knead on floured surface for 10 minutes or until smooth and elastic. Let rise, covered, for 20 minutes. Divide into 4 portions; divide each portion into 6 pieces. Shape each into ball. Roll each into 5-inch circle on lightly floured surface. Place on baking sheet. Let rise, covered, for 30 minutes. Bake at 500 degrees for 5 minutes or until puffed and tops just begin to brown. Remove to wire rack to cool.
Yield: 24 servings.

Approx Per Serving: Cal 112; Prot 4 g; Carbo 21 g; Fiber 3 g;
     T Fat 2 g; Chol 0 mg; Sod 82 mg.

Dietary Exchanges: Bread/Starch 1 1/2

Desserts

MICROWAVE SPICED APPLE CRISP

4 medium apples, peeled
1/3 cup orange juice
1/4 teaspoon grated orange
  rind

1 teaspoon cinnamon
3 tablespoons dark brown
  sugar
1/4 cup crushed gingersnaps

Slice apples into 1/4-inch rings. Arrange in 10-inch glass pie plate. Drizzle with orange juice. Mix orange rind, cinnamon and brown sugar in small bowl. Sprinkle over apples. Microwave, loosely covered with waxed paper, on High for 3 to 4 minutes or until apples are tender, rotating dish after 2 minutes. Top with gingersnaps. Serve immediately. Yield: 4 servings.

Approx Per Serving: Cal 158; Prot 1 g; Carbo 36 g; Fiber 3 g;
   T Fat 2 g; Chol 0 mg; Sod 26 mg.

Dietary Exchanges: Fruit 1 1/2; Bread/Starch 1/2; Fat 1/2

BANANA AND PINEAPPLE PUDDING

3/4 sponge cake
3 large bananas
2 small packages sugar-free
  vanilla instant pudding mix

1 16-ounce can crushed
   pineapple, drained
12 ounces whipped topping

Tear sponge cake into bite-sized pieces. Slice bananas. Prepare pudding mix using package directions. Fold pineapple into pudding. Layer sponge cake, bananas, pudding and whipped topping 1/2 at a time in large bowl. Chill until serving time. May substitute vanilla wafers for sponge cake. Yield: 24 servings.

Approx Per Serving: Cal 263; Prot 8 g; Carbo 43 g; Fiber <1 g;
   T Fat 7 g; Chol 92 mg; Sod 633 mg.

Dietary Exchanges: Fruit 1/2; Bread/Starch 2 1/2; Fat 1 1/2

BANANA SPLIT DESSERT

1 small package sugar-free
  vanilla instant pudding mix
3 cups skim milk
8 2½-inch graham crackers
½ cup drained crushed
  pineapple

1 banana, sliced
1 cup sliced strawberries
1 cup whipped topping

Prepare pudding mix with skim milk, using package directions. Layer graham crackers, pudding, pineapple, banana, strawberries and whipped topping in 8x8-inch dish. Chill for 1 hour or longer. Yield: 6 servings.

Approx Per Serving: Cal 204; Prot 5 g; Carbo 39 g; Fiber 2 g;
    T Fat 4 g; Chol 2 mg; Sod 407 mg.

Dietary Exchanges: Milk ½; Fruit 1; Bread/Starch 1; Fat 1

BLACKBERRY COBBLER

2 pounds blackberries
⅔ cup packed brown sugar
1 teaspoon cinnamon

1 16-ounce package nut
  bread mix
2 egg whites

Spread blackberries in 9x11-inch baking dish sprayed with non-stick cooking spray. Sprinkle with brown sugar and cinnamon. Prepare nut bread mix using package directions, substituting egg whites for whole egg and omitting oil. Pour over berries. Bake at 400 degrees for 1 hour and 5 minutes or until toothpick inserted in center comes out clean. May substitute other berries for blackberries.
Yield: 12 servings.

Approx Per Serving: Cal 87; Prot 1 g; Carbo 21 g; Fiber 5 g;
    T Fat <1 g; Chol 0 mg; Sod 12 mg.
    Nutritional information does not include bread mix.

Dietary Exchanges: Fruit 1

☎ Make a **Blueberry Sauce** by blending ½ cup sugar, 2 teaspoons cornstarch, ½ cup water and 1 tablespoon lemon juice in saucepan, stirring in 2 cups fresh or frozen blueberries and then cooking over medium heat until thickened, stirring constantly. Serve over cake, ice cream, puddings, pancakes or cheesecake.

BLUEBERRY-GRAPE COMPOTE

¹/₄ cup sugar
¹/₄ cup water
¹/₂ teaspoon grated lime rind
¹/₄ cup lime juice

2 cups blueberries
2 cups seedless grape halves
2 kiwifruit, peeled, sliced

Combine sugar, water and lime rind in saucepan; mix well. Cook over medium heat until sugar dissolves, stirring frequently. Stir in lime juice. Cool to room temperature. Combine with blueberries and grapes in bowl; mix well. Chill, covered, until serving time, stirring occasionally. Top with kiwifruit at serving time. Yield: 6 servings.

Approx Per Serving: Cal 95; Prot 1 g; Carbo 25 g; Fiber 3 g;
    T Fat <1 g; Chol 0 mg; Sod 5 mg.

Dietary Exchanges: Fruit 1

DIET CHEESECAKE

28 ounces low-fat cottage
    cheese
2 tablespoons lemon juice
3 tablespoons flour

3 eggs
³/₄ cup sugar
¹/₂ cup confectioners' sugar
¹/₈ teaspoon vanilla extract

Combine cottage cheese, lemon juice, flour, eggs, sugar, confectioners' sugar and vanilla in blender container. Process until smooth. Pour into 9-inch springform pan sprayed with nonstick cooking spray. Bake at 325 degrees for 35 to 40 minutes or until set. Cool to room temperature. Store in refrigerator. Place on serving plate; remove side of pan. Yield: 12 servings.

Approx Per Serving: Cal 151; Prot 11 g; Carbo 21 g; Fiber <1 g;
    T Fat 3 g; Chol 74 mg; Sod 286 mg.

Dietary Exchanges: Meat 1¹/₂

1970

ICYCLICLES

1 cup low-fat yogurt
Vanilla extract to taste

1 6-ounce can frozen orange
  juice concentrate, thawed

Combine yogurt, vanilla and orange juice concentrate in bowl; mix well. Fill 3-ounce paper cups 3/4 full. Freeze until slushy. Insert wooden sticks into cups for handles. Freeze until firm. Peel off paper cups to serve. Yield: 5 servings.

Approx Per Serving: Cal 83; Prot 3 g; Carbo 16 g; Fiber <1 g;
   T Fat <1 g; Chol 3 mg; Sod 33 mg.

Dietary Exchanges: Milk 1/2; Fruit 1

SPECIAL ICE CREAM

6 egg whites
Salt to taste
3/4 cup sugar

8 ounces whipped topping
1 teaspoon vanilla extract

Beat egg whites with salt in mixer bowl until frothy. Add sugar 2 tablespoons at a time, beating constantly until stiff peaks form. Fold in whipped topping and vanilla gently. Spoon into freezer container. Freeze for 4 hours or longer. Yield: 8 servings.

Approx Per Serving: Cal 154; Prot 3 g; Carbo 22 g; Fiber 0 g;
   T Fat 6 g; Chol 22 mg; Sod 75 mg.

Dietary Exchanges: Meat 1/2; Fat 2

PEACH DAIQUIRI ICE

1 16-ounce can juice-pack
  sliced peaches
1/4 cup sugar
2 tablespoons rum

1/4 teaspoon finely grated
  lime rind
2 tablespoons lime juice

Drain peaches, reserving 2 tablespoons juice. Combine peaches, sugar, rum, lime rind, lime juice and reserved peach juice in blender container or food processor container; process until smooth. Pour into 4x8-inch loaf pan. Freeze, covered, for 4 hours or until firm. Let stand for 5 minutes before serving. Yield: 4 servings.

Approx Per Serving: Cal 90; Prot <1 g; Carbo 20 g; Fiber <1 g;
   T Fat <1 g; Chol 0 mg; Sod 4 mg.

Dietary Exchanges: Fruit 1/2

FROZEN RASPBERRY DESSERT

1 cup flour
1/2 cup packed light brown
  sugar
1/2 cup chopped walnuts
1/2 cup margarine, softened
2 egg whites

1/2 cup sugar
1 10-ounce package frozen
  raspberries
2 teaspoons lemon juice
3 cups whipped topping

Combine flour, brown sugar, walnuts and margarine in bowl; mix well. Pat 1/4 inch thick on ungreased baking sheet. Bake at 350 degrees for 20 minutes or until crumbly, stirring every 5 minutes. Cool and crumble. Sprinkle half the crumbs into 9x13-inch baking dish. Beat egg whites in bowl until frothy. Add sugar gradually, beating constantly until stiff peaks form. Stir in raspberries and lemon juice. Fold in whipped topping. Spread in prepared pan. Top with remaining crumbs. Freeze until serving time. Yield: 16 servings.

Approx Per Serving: Cal 229; Prot 4 g; Carbo 29 g; Fiber 1 g;
  T Fat 11 g; Chol 1 mg; Sod 95 mg.

Dietary Exchanges: Fruit 1/2; Bread/Starch 1/2; Fat 2 1/2

SPICED FRUIT CASSEROLE

1 17-ounce can apricot
  halves
1 16-ounce can peach halves
1 16-ounce can pear halves
1 15-ounce can pineapple
  chunks
1 16-ounce can white
  cherries

1 cup orange juice
1/3 cup packed brown sugar
1 tablespoon lemon juice
1 3-inch cinnamon stick
4 whole cloves
1/8 teaspoon mace

Drain fruit; cut apricots, peaches and pears halves into halves. Layer fruit in 3-quart baking dish. Combine orange juice, brown sugar, lemon juice, cinnamon, cloves and mace in saucepan. Bring to a boil; reduce heat. Simmer for 2 minutes. Pour over fruit. Bake at 350 degrees for 30 minutes. Cool to room temperature. Chill, covered, for 8 hours. Remove cinnamon stick and cloves. Serve cold or reheat. Yield: 20 servings.

Approx Per Serving: Cal 76; Prot 1 g; Carbo 20 g; Fiber 1 g;
  T Fat <1 g; Chol 0 mg; Sod 5 mg.

Dietary Exchanges: Fruit 1

ORANGE PUMPKIN MOUSSE

3 tablespoons margarine
1½ cups mashed cooked
  pumpkin
⅔ cup sugar
¼ teaspoon cinnamon
½ teaspoon allspice

½ cup evaporated skim milk
½ cup egg substitute
1 3-ounce package orange
  gelatin
1 cup boiling water
¼ cup chopped pecans

Melt margarine in heavy saucepan. Stir in pumpkin, sugar, cinnamon, allspice, skim milk and egg substitute; mix well. Bring to a boil over low heat, stirring constantly. Chill in refrigerator. Dissolve orange gelatin in boiling water in bowl. Chill until slightly thickened. Set bowl in large bowl of ice and water. Beat until light and fluffy. Fold in chilled pumpkin mixture. Spoon into serving bowl. Sprinkle with pecans. Chill until serving time. Yield: 8 servings.

Approx Per Serving: Cal 200; Prot 5 g; Carbo 31 g; Fiber <1 g;
  T Fat 7 g; Chol 1 mg; Sod 132 mg.

Dietary Exchanges: Bread/Starch 1; Meat ½; Fat 1½

PAVLOVA

2 egg whites
¾ cup sugar
1 teaspoon cornstarch

½ teaspoon baking powder
1 teaspoon vanilla extract
1 teaspoon vinegar

Beat egg whites in mixer bowl until stiff peaks form. Fold in sugar, cornstarch, baking powder, vanilla and vinegar. Moisten bottom of 8-inch round baking pan. Line with waxed paper cut to fit pan. Spoon egg whites into prepared pan. Bake on bottom shelf of oven preheated to 275 degrees for 1 hour. Turn off oven. Let meringue stand in closed oven for 15 minutes. Place on serving plate. Fill with fresh fruit. Yield: 6 servings.

Approx Per Serving: Cal 100; Prot 1 g; Carbo 25 g; Fiber 0 g;
  T Fat 0 g; Chol 0 mg; Sod 45 mg.

Dietary Exchanges: None (Because of sugar content, not
  recommended for diabetics.)

MICROWAVE MAPLE PEARS

3 medium firm pears
1 tablespoon lemon juice
2 tablespoons maple syrup
Nutmeg to taste

1/3 cup low-fat ricotta cheese
2 teaspoons grated lemon
  rind
2 teaspoons maple syrup

Cut pears into halves lengthwise, leaving stem attached to 1 half. Remove core carefully from each half with melon baller. Arrange cut side up in 10-inch glass pie plate with wide end toward outer edge. Drizzle with lemon juice. Spoon 2 teaspoons maple syrup into each cored center; sprinkle with nutmeg. Microwave on High for 7 minutes or until pears are tender, rotating dish after 5 minutes. Spoon juices from cores over cut edges of pears. Top with mixture of ricotta cheese and lemon rind. Drizzle with remaining 2 teaspoons syrup. Serve warm or at room temperature. Yield: 6 servings.

Approx Per Serving: Cal 91; Prot 2 g; Carbo 19 g; Fiber 2 g;
    T Fat 1 g; Chol 4 mg; Sod 19 mg.

Dietary Exchanges: Fruit 1; Bread/Starch 1/2; Meat 1/2

GRANOLA STRAWBERRIES

1 cup oats
1 cup wheat germ
1/2 cup graham cracker
  crumbs
1/2 cup slivered blanched
  almonds

1/2 cup coconut
2 tablespoons light brown
  sugar
1 teaspoon vanilla extract
3 cups milk
4 1/2 cups strawberries

Combine oats, wheat germ, cracker crumbs, almonds, coconut, brown sugar and vanilla in shallow baking pan; mix well. Bake at 275 degrees for 1 hour, stirring occasionally. Cool to room temperature. Store in airtight container. Combine with milk and strawberries in bowl; mix gently. Yield: 6 servings.

Approx Per Serving: Cal 182; Prot 8 g; Carbo 23 g; Fiber 3 g;
    T Fat 8 g; Chol 8 mg; Sod 54 mg.

Dietary Exchanges: Milk 1/2; Fruit 1/2; Bread/Starch 1; Fat 1 1/2

ANGEL FOOD CAKE

1½ cups egg whites, at room
    temperature
1½ teaspoons cream of tartar
1 teaspoon vanilla extract

1 cup sugar
1½ cups sifted
    confectioners' sugar
1 cup sifted cake flour

Beat egg whites, cream of tartar and vanilla in 3-quart mixer bowl at medium speed until soft peaks form. Add sugar 2 tablespoons at a time, beating constantly until stiff peaks form. Sift confectioners' sugar and flour together 3 times. Sift ¼ at a time over egg whites, folding in gently with rubber spatula. Spoon into ungreased 10-inch tube pan. Cut through batter with knife. Bake in preheated 350-degree oven for 40 minutes or until top springs back when touched lightly. Invert on funnel to cool. Loosen cake from side of pan with knife. Remove to serving plate. Yield: 12 servings.

Approx Per Serving: Cal 164; Prot 4 g; Carbo 38 g; Fiber <1 g;
    T Fat <1 g; Chol 0 mg; Sod 50 mg.

Dietary Exchanges: Bread/Starch ½; Meat ½

LEMON CHIFFON CAKE

5 egg whites, at room
    temperature
2 tablespoons sifted
    confectioners' sugar
1½ cups sifted cake flour
1 cup sugar

2 teaspoons baking powder
¼ teaspoon salt
½ cup oil
Grated rind of 2 lemons
½ cup fresh lemon juice

Beat egg whites with confectioners' sugar in large mixer bowl just until stiff peaks form. Sift flour, sugar, baking powder and salt into medium mixer bowl. Make well in center. Add oil, lemon rind and juice. Beat at medium speed until smooth. Fold gently into egg whites. Spoon into ungreased 9-inch tube pan. Bake at 350 degrees for 35 minutes or until golden brown. Cool in pan for 5 minutes. Invert onto wire rack to cool completely. Yield: 16 servings.

Approx Per Serving: Cal 149; Prot 2 g; Carbo 21 g; Fiber <1 g;
    T Fat 7 g; Chol 0 mg; Sod 89 mg.

Dietary Exchanges: Bread/Starch ½; Fat 1½

LEMON POUND CAKE

1 2-layer package Duncan
   Hines lemon supreme cake
   mix
1 4-ounce package lemon
   instant pudding mix

1 cup water
⅓ cup oil
1 cup egg substitute

Combine all ingredients in large mixer bowl. Beat at low speed until blended. Beat at medium speed for 2 minutes. Spoon into greased and floured bundt pan. Bake at 350 degrees for 55 minutes. Cool in pan for 25 minutes. Invert onto serving plate. May make chocolate pound cake with Duncan Hines chocolate cake mix and chocolate instant pudding mix. Yield: 16 servings.

Approx Per Serving: Cal 293; Prot 4 g; Carbo 48 g; Fiber <1 g;
   T Fat 9 g; Chol <1 mg; Sod 382 mg.

Dietary Exchanges: Bread/Starch 3; Meat ½; Fat 2

FROSTED ORANGE CARROT CAKE

1 cup molasses
1 cup margarine, softened
Egg substitute to equal 4
   eggs
½ cup orange juice
1 cup all-purpose flour
1 cup whole wheat flour
2 teaspoons soda
1 teaspoon cinnamon

½ teaspoon salt
2 cups shredded carrots
½ cup chopped walnuts
3 ounces Neufchâtel cheese,
   softened
2 tablespoons margarine,
   softened
1½ cups confectioners' sugar
1 teaspoon grated orange rind

Combine molasses, 1 cup margarine, egg substitute and orange juice in bowl; mix well. Sift in all-purpose flour, whole wheat flour, soda, cinnamon and salt; mix well. Stir in carrots and walnuts. Spoon into 2 greased and floured 8 or 9-inch cake pans. Bake at 350 degrees for 30 to 35 minutes or until layers test done. Cool in pans for 10 minutes. Remove to wire racks to cool completely. Combine Neufchâtel cheese and 2 tablespoons margarine in bowl; mix until smooth. Add confectioners' sugar and orange rind; mix well. Spread between layers and over top and side of cake. Garnish with additional grated orange rind or toasted chopped walnuts. Yield: 12 servings.

Approx Per Serving: Cal 397; Prot 5 g; Carbo 48 g; Fiber 2 g;
   T Fat 21 g; Chol 6 mg; Sod 493 mg.

Dietary Exchanges: Vegetable ½; Bread/Starch 1; Meat ½; Fat 4½

APPLE PEANUT BUTTER COOKIES

3 cups flour
1/2 teaspoon soda
1/2 teaspoon salt
1 cup shortening
1 cup sugar
1 1/2 cups packed brown sugar

1 cup peanut butter
1 cup applesauce
2 eggs
1 teaspoon vanilla extract
1 cup chopped raisins

Sift flour, soda and salt together. Cream shortening, sugar, brown sugar and peanut butter in mixer bowl until light and fluffy. Combine applesauce, eggs and vanilla in bowl; mix well. Add to creamed mixture alternately with dry ingredients, mixing well after each addition. Stir in raisins. Drop by rounded teaspoonfuls onto greased cookie sheet. Bake at 350 degrees for 10 to 12 minutes or until light brown. Remove to wire rack to cool. Yield: 54 servings.

Approx Per Serving: Cal 138; Prot 2 g; Carbo 19 g; Fiber 1 g;
     T Fat 7 g; Chol 10 mg; Sod 53 mg.

Dietary Exchanges: Bread/Starch 1/2; Fat 1 1/2

BANANA COOKIES

1 1/2 cups sifted flour
1 cup sugar
1/2 teaspoon soda
1/4 teaspoon nutmeg
3/4 teaspoon cinnamon
3/4 cup shortening

1 egg, beaten
1 cup mashed banana
1 teaspoon vanilla extract
1 3/4 cups oats
1/2 cup chopped walnuts

Sift flour, sugar, soda, nutmeg and cinnamon into bowl. Cut in shortening until crumbly. Add egg, banana, vanilla, oats and walnuts; mix well. Drop by teaspoonfuls 1 1/2 inches apart onto ungreased cookie sheet. Bake at 350 degrees for 10 minutes or until edges are brown. Remove to wire rack to cool. Yield: 42 servings.

Approx Per Serving: Cal 91; Prot 1 g; Carbo 12 g; Fiber <1 g;
     T Fat 5 g; Chol 7 mg; Sod 12 mg.

Dietary Exchanges: Bread/Starch 1/2; Fat 1

BUTTERSCOTCH BROWNIES

1/4 cup oil
1 cup packed light brown
  sugar
2 egg whites

3/4 cup sifted flour
1 teaspoon baking powder
1/2 teaspoon vanilla extract
1/2 cup chopped pecans

Blend oil and brown sugar in bowl. Stir in egg whites. Sift in flour and baking powder; mix well. Stir in vanilla and pecans. Spoon into oiled 8x8-inch baking pan. Bake at 350 degrees for 25 minutes; do not overbake. Cool on wire rack. Cut into squares. Yield: 32 servings.

Approx Per Serving: Cal 63; Prot 1 g; Carbo 9 g; Fiber <1 g;
  T Fat 3 g; Chol 0 mg; Sod 16 mg.

Dietary Exchanges: Fat 1/2

OATMEAL BROWNIES

2/3 cup sugar
1/3 cup water
3 tablespoons oil
1/2 teaspoon vanilla extract
2 egg whites, lightly beaten
1/2 cup flour

1/3 cup quick-cooking oats
1/4 cup baking cocoa
3/4 teaspoon baking powder
1/8 teaspoon salt
1 teaspoon sifted
  confectioners' sugar

Combine sugar, water, oil and vanilla in medium bowl; mix well. Blend in egg whites. Add mixture of flour, oats, cocoa, baking powder and salt; mix well. Spoon into 8x8-inch baking pan sprayed with nonstick cooking spray. Bake at 350 degrees for 23 minutes or until wooden pick comes out clean. Cool on wire rack. Sprinkle with confectioners' sugar. Cut into 2x2½-inch bars. Yield: 12 servings.

Approx Per Serving: Cal 106; Prot 2 g; Carbo 17 g; Fiber 1 g;
  T Fat 4 g; Chol 0 mg; Sod 29 mg.

Dietary Exchanges: Bread/Starch 1/2; Fat 1

☎ Reduce the amount of nuts in cookies or omit nuts entirely to reduce calories and fat. Substitute low-calorie cereals for crunch.

MUDBALL COOKIES

6 tablespoons baking cocoa
2 tablespoons melted
  margarine
3 cups oats
¾ cup nonfat dry milk

1 cup corn syrup
½ cup chunky peanut butter
2 teaspoons vanilla extract
½ teaspoon salt
½ cup seedless raisins

Combine cocoa, margarine, oats, dry milk, corn syrup, peanut butter, vanilla, salt and raisins in large bowl; mix well. Shape into balls. Store in airtight container at room temperature or in freezer. May press into 8x8-inch dish and cut into squares if preferred. Yield: 36 servings.

Approx Per Serving: Cal 94; Prot 3 g; Carbo 15 g; Fiber 1 g;
    T Fat 3 g; Chol <1 mg; Sod 67 mg.

Dietary Exchanges: Bread/Starch ½; Fat ½

FRESH LEMON COOKIES

1 cup flour
2 teaspoons baking powder
⅛ teaspoon salt
2 tablespoons margarine,
  softened
½ cup sugar

1 egg
1 tablespoon grated lemon
  rind
2 tablespoons fresh lemon
  juice

Mix flour, baking powder and salt in small bowl. Cream margarine in mixer bowl until light. Add sugar gradually, beating until fluffy. Add egg, lemon rind and lemon juice; mix well. Stir in dry ingredients. Drop by heaping teaspoonfuls onto cookie sheet lightly sprayed with nonstick cooking spray. Bake at 350 degrees for 10 minutes or until edges are light brown. Cool slightly on cookie sheet. Remove to wire rack to cool completely. Yield: 28 servings.

Approx Per Serving: Cal 40; Prot 1 g; Carbo 7 g; Fiber <1 g;
    T Fat 1 g; Chol 10 mg; Sod 45 mg.

Dietary Exchanges: Bread/Starch ½

☎ Bake cakes or cookies in 9x13-inch or 10x15-inch pans when possible, then cut into small portions. Smaller portions are just as delicious but yield fewer calories, carbohydrates and fats.

OATCAKES

2½ cups oats
⅔ cup (or less) sugar
½ cup flour
¼ teaspoon soda
1 teaspoon salt
¾ cup lard
¼ cup (or less) cold water
½ cup crushed bran flakes

 Mix oats, sugar, flour, soda and salt in bowl. Cut in lard until crumbly. Mix with hands until smooth. Add just enough water to form ball. Roll ¼ inch thick on surface coated with bran flake crumbs. Cut into circles or squares; place on ungreased cookie sheet. Bake at 375 degrees for 12 to 15 minutes or until light brown. Remove to wire rack to cool. This recipe, from a restaurant in Nova Scotia, calls for lard. Health-conscious cooks may want to try it with vegetable shortening. Yield: 36 servings.

Approx Per Serving: Cal 82; Prot 1 g; Carbo 9 g; Fiber <1 g;
 T Fat 5 g; Chol 4 mg; Sod 66 mg.

Dietary Exchanges: Bread/Starch ½; Fat 1

RAISIN OAT BRAN COOKIES

1 cup ralsins
½ cup dark corn syrup
2 cups oat bran
2 cups oats
½ cup barley flour
1 teaspoon soda
1 teaspoon cinnamon
½ cup margarine, softened
¾ cup packed brown sugar
1 teaspoon vanilla extract
2 egg whites
1 cup unsweetened
 applesauce

 Combine raisins and corn syrup in bowl; let stand for 10 to 15 minutes. Combine oat bran, oats, barley flour, soda and cinnamon in bowl. Cream margarine, brown sugar and vanilla in mixer bowl until light and fluffy. Blend in egg whites and applesauce. Add dry ingredients and raisin mixture; mix well. Drop by teaspoonfuls onto greased cookie sheet. Press with fork to flatten. Bake at 375 degrees for 12 minutes or until golden brown. Remove to wire rack to cool. May substitute whole wheat flour for barley flour. Yield: 48 servings

Approx Per Serving: Cal 78; Prot 2 g; Carbo 15 g; Fiber 1 g;
 T Fat 2 g; Chol 0 mg; Sod 46 mg.

Dietary Exchanges: Bread/Starch ½; Fat ½

SPICY WHEAT COOKIES

1/4 cup oil
1/4 cup packed brown sugar
1 egg white
2 tablespoons plus 2
    teaspoons unsweetened
    orange juice
1 cup whole wheat flour

1/4 cup wheat germ
1/2 teaspoon soda
1/2 teaspoon cinnamon
1/4 teaspoon nutmeg
1/8 teaspoon cloves
1/8 teaspoon salt
1/4 cup raisins

Blend oil and brown sugar in medium bowl. Add egg white and orange juice; mix well. Mix flour, wheat germ, soda, cinnamon, nutmeg, cloves and salt in small bowl. Add to oil mixture, mixing well. Stir in raisins. Drop by rounded teaspoonfuls 2 inches apart onto ungreased cookie sheet. Bake at 350 degrees for 10 minutes or until light brown. Remove to wire rack to cool. Yield: 30 servings.

Approx Per Serving: Cal 45; Prot 1 g; Carbo 6 g; Fiber 1 g;
    T Fat 2 g; Chol 0 mg; Sod 24 mg.

Dietary Exchanges: Bread/Starch 1/2; Fat 1/2

☎ Make a very easy but elegant **Coeur à la Creme** by pressing 1 pound cream-style cottage cheese through a sieve. Blend in 2 tablespoons sugar and 1/2 teaspoon vanilla. Line a small colander or a small wire basket of any shape with several layers of moist cheesecloth. Spoon sieved cottage cheese into basket; press gently. Fold cheesecloth over cheese and invert small plate on top for pressure. Place basket over bowl to catch dripping moisture. Chill overnight. Remove plate and open cheesecloth. Invert onto serving plate and remove cheesecloth carefully. Serve with fresh fruit, crisp cookies or thinly sliced pound cake.

PIES

LIME PIE

1 cup evaporated skim milk
4 teaspoons cornstarch
1½ cups water
1 small package sugar-free
  lime gelatin

2 tablespoons lemon juice
4 packets artificial sweetener
¼ teaspoon cream of tartar
1 graham cracker pie shell

Freeze evaporated milk until slushy. Blend cornstarch and water in saucepan. Cook until thickened, stirring constantly. Stir in gelatin until dissolved. Add lemon juice and sweetener. Beat evaporated milk with cream of tartar in mixer bowl until stiff peaks form. Fold in lemon mixture. Spoon into pie shell. Chill until serving time. Yield: 6 servings.

Approx Per Serving: Cal 316; Prot 6 g; Carbo 41 g; Fiber <1 g;
    T Fat 15 g; Chol 2 mg; Sod 367 mg.

Dietary Exchanges: Milk ½; Bread/Starch 2½; Fat 3

SVELTE STRAWBERRY PIE

1 3-ounce package sugar-
   free strawberry gelatin
1 3-ounce package sugar-
   free vanilla pudding mix

1¼ cups water
1 quart fresh strawberries
1 baked 9-inch pie shell

Combine gelatin, pudding mix and water in saucepan; mix well. Cook until thickened, stirring constantly. Cool to room temperature. Add strawberries; mix gently. Spoon into pie shell. Chill in refrigerator. Let stand at room temperature for 30 minutes before serving. Serve with whipped topping. May add artificial sweetener to taste if desired. Yield: 8 servings.

Approx Per Serving: Cal 158; Prot 2 g; Carbo 20 g; Fiber 2 g;
    T Fat 8 g; Chol 0 mg; Sod 357 mg.

Dietary Exchanges: Fruit ½; Bread/Starch 1; Fat 1½

Special Helps

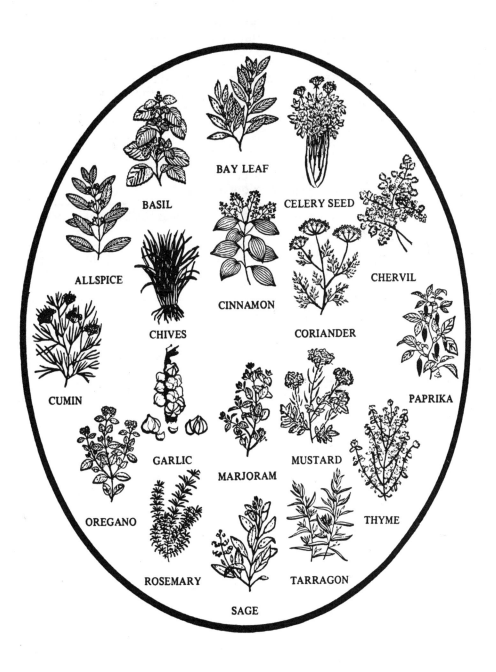

BASIL

BAY LEAF

CELERY SEED

ALLSPICE

CINNAMON

CHERVIL

CHIVES

CORIANDER

CUMIN

GARLIC

MARJORAM

MUSTARD

PAPRIKA

OREGANO

ROSEMARY

SAGE

TARRAGON

THYME

HERBS AND SPICES

Allspice	Pungent aromatic spice, whole or in powdered form. It is excellent in marinades, particularly in game marinade, or in curries.
Basil	Can be chopped and added to cold poultry salads. If the recipe calls for tomatoes or tomato sauce, add a touch of basil to bring out a rich flavor.
Bay leaf	The basis of many French seasonings. It is added to soups, stews, marinades and stuffings.
Chervil	One of the traditional *fines herbes* used in French-derived cooking. (The others are tarragon, parsley and chives.) It is good in omelets or soups.
Chives	Available fresh, dried or frozen, it can be substituted for raw onion or shallot in any poultry recipe.
Cinnamon	Ground from the bark of the cinnamon tree, it is important in desserts as well as savory dishes.
Coriander	Adds an unusual flavor to soups, stews, chili dishes, curries and some desserts.
Cumin	A staple spice in Mexican cooking. To use, rub seeds together and let them fall into the dish just before serving. Cumin also comes in powdered form.
Garlic	One of the oldest herbs in the world, it must be carefully handled. For best results, press or crush garlic clove.
Marjoram	An aromatic herb of the mint family, it is good in soups, sauces, stuffings and stews.
Mustard (dry)	Brings a sharp bite to sauces. Sprinkle just a touch over roast chicken for a delightful flavor treat.
Oregano	A staple herb in Italian, Spanish and Mexican cuisines. It is very good in dishes with a tomato foundation; it adds an excellent savory taste.
Paprika	A mild pepper that adds color to many dishes. The very best paprika is imported from Hungary.
Rosemary	A tasty herb important in seasoning stuffing for duck, partridge, capon and other poultry.
Sage	A perennial favorite with all kinds of poultry and stuffings. It is particularly good with goose.
Tarragon	One of the *fines herbes*. Goes well with all poultry dishes whether hot or cold.
Thyme	Usually used with bay leaf in soups, stews and sauces.

THE WELL-BALANCED DIET

Everyone has heard of the "balanced diet" but would be hard pressed to explain it in detail or possibly even name the Food Groups. Examine the following chart. It shows what is necessary to meet the daily nutritional needs of a healthy individual. Test yourself to see how *your* diet stands up. Remember that fewer than the recommended servings may show that your diet is lacking but more servings may not necessarily be a plus if they lead to excess calories, fat, cholesterol and sodium.

Food Group	Daily Requirement
Vegetables and Fruits: *Serving size:* 1/2 cup juice, fruit or vegetable or 1 piece medium fruit or 1/4 cup dried fruit	4 servings (Include citrus daily for Vitamin C and dark green or orange vegetables and fruits which are high in Vitamin A 3 or 4 times a week.
Breads and Starches: *Serving size:* 1 slice bread or 1/2 cup cooked cereal, macaroni, noodles or rice or 1 ounce ready-to-eat cereal	4 servings (Choose whole grain or enriched breads and grain products.)
Dairy Products: *Serving size:* 1 cup milk or yogurt or 1 ounce cheese or 1/2 cup cottage cheese	Children: 3 servings Teenagers: 4 servings Adults: 2 servings Pregnant Women: 4 servings Nursing Mothers: 4 servings
Meats: *Serving size:* 2 to 3 ounces cooked lean meat, fish or poultry or 2 eggs or 1 cup dried beans, peas or lentils	All Ages: 2 servings Pregnant Women: 3 servings
Fats:	Minimal amounts of healthy fats.
Sweets:	None recommended.

DIETARY EXCHANGES

The exchange system of diet monitoring is a relatively new addition to diet control. This system first developed to assist diabetic patients in controlling the strict diets they needed while giving them as much flexibility in their choices as was possible. Weight management groups such as Weight Watchers have since adopted the system.

We are pleased to provide Dietary Exchanges for recipes in this book. This chart will help you understand and use that information. Notice that some foods must count as Fat Exchanges (Fat Exch.) also.

Milk Exchanges

One milk exchange contains 12 grams of carbohydrate, 8 grams of protein, a trace of fat and about 80 calories. Skim milk has about 80 calories per exchange (half the calories of whole milk).

Whole milk (+2 fat exch.) . . . . .1 cup	Skim milk . . . . .1 cup
Evaporated skim milk	Nonfat dry milk powder . . . . . 1/3 cup
(+2 fat exch.) . . . . 1/2 cup	Yogurt, plain from skim milk . . .1 cup
Buttermilk (+2 fat exch.) . . . . .1 cup	Yogurt, plain from 2% milk
1% milk (+1/2 fat exch.) . . . . . .1 cup	(+1 fat exch.) . . . . .1 cup
2% milk (+1 fat exch.) . . . . . . .1 cup	

Low-Carbohydrate Vegetable Exchanges

One low-carbohydrate vegetable exchange contains about 5 grams of carbohydrate, 2 grams of protein and 25 calories. One-half cup (raw or cooked, with no fat added) is considered one exchange.

Asparagus	Cabbage	Eggplant	Green beans
Bean sprouts	Carrots	Green pepper	Summer squash
Beets	Cauliflower	Mushrooms	Tomatoes
Broccoli	Celery	Okra	Turnips
Brussels sprouts	Cucumbers	Onions	Vegetable juice

Fruit Exchanges

One fruit exchange contains about 10 grams of carbohydrate and 40 calories. No sugar added.

Apple . . . . .1 small	Dates 2
Apple juice . . . . 1/3 cup	Figs, fresh or dried 1
Apricots, fresh . . . . 2 medium	Grapefruit 1/2
Apricots, dried . . . . 4 halves	Grapefruit juice . . . . 1/2 cup
Banana . . . . 1/2 small	Grapes 12
Blueberries and Raspberries . . 1/2 cup	Grape juice . . . . 1/4 cup
Strawberries . . . . 3/4 cup	Pear . . . . .1 small
Cantaloupe . . . . 1/4 small	Pineapple, fresh . . . . 1/2 cup
Watermelon . . . . .1 cup	Pineapple juice . . . . 1/3 cup
Orange . . . . .1 small	Plums . . . . 2 medium
Orange juice . . . . 1/2 cup	Prunes . . . . 2 medium
Peach . . . . 1 medium	Prune juice . . . . 1/4 cup
Cherries . . . . 10 large	Raisins . . . . .2 tablespoons

Bread/Starch Exchanges

Including breads, cereals, grains, pasta, high-carbohydrate vegetables and other primarily carbohydrate foods. One bread exchange contains 15 grams of carbohydrate, 2 grams of protein and about 70 calories.

Bread . . . . .1 slice	Pasta (without sauce) . . . . . . ½ cup
Bagel . . . . ½	Rice, cooked . . . . ½ cup
Biscuit (2 inch diameter) (+1 fat exch.) .1	Grits, cooked . . . . ½ cup
Corn muffin (+1 fat exch.) . . . 1 piece	Sponge cake, plain (1½ cube) . 1 piece
Hamburger or frankfurter bun . . . . ½	Baked beans, no pork . . . . . . ¼ cup
Muffin (2 inch diameter)	Cooked, dried beans . . . . . . ½ cup
(+1 fat exch.) 1	Corn . . . . ⅓ cup
Muffin, English . . . . ½	Parsnips . . . . ½ cup
Tortilla (6 inch diameter) 1	Pumpkin, unsweetened . . . . . ¾ cup
Cereal, cooked . . . . .½ cup	Popcorn (popped, no fat) . .about 3 cups
Cereal, dry . . . . ¾ cup	Potatoes, white, baked . . . . . 1 small
Crackers, saltines 6	Potatoes, white, mashed . . . . ½ cup
Crackers, graham 2	Potatoes, French-fried . . . . 6 pieces
Pretzels (ring, medium) 6	(½ inch by ½ inch by 2 inches)
Flour . . . . .2½ tablespoons	(+ 1 fat exch.)
Cornmeal . . . . 2 tablespoons	Potato chips (+2 fat exch.) 15
Bread stuffing (+ 1 fat exch.) . . .½ cup	Sweet potatoes, unsweetened . ¼ cup

Meat Exchanges (and Other Protein-Rich Foods)

One meat exchange if 1 ounce lean meat contains 7 grams protein, 3 grams fat and about 55 calories. The following amounts average one meat exchange.

Meat and poultry: (lean) . . . .1 ounce	Sardines, drained 3
Beef, chicken, lamb, pork	Canned salmon, tuna, crab
Turkey and game	lobster . . . . ¼ cup
Cold cuts/luncheon meats . . .1 ounce	Egg . . . . .1 medium
Frankfurters, (8 to 9 per pound) 1	Cheese, Cheddar, Swiss
Sausage patty, (7 patties per pound) . .1	American . . . . .1 ounce
Sausage links	Cheese, cottage . . . . ¼ cup
(2½ inches by ½ inch) 1	Cheese, Roquefort, Parmesan . ¼ cup
Liver, heart, kidney . . . . . . .1 ounce	Peanut butter
Fish and seafood:	(+ 2 fat exch.) . . . . . 2 tablespoons
Haddock and similar fish . . .1 ounce	Dried beans and peas
Clams, oysters, shrimp, scallops . .5	(+ 1 bread exch.) . . . . ½ cup

Fat Exchanges

One exchange of fat contains 5 grams of fat and about 45 calories.

Avocado (4 inch diameter) . . . . . . ⅛	Bacon, crisp-fried . . . . 1 slice
Oil . . . . .1 teaspoon	Cream, light . . . . 2 tablespoons
Olives . . . . 5 small	Cream, sour . . . . 2 tablespoons
Nuts . . . . 6 small	French salad dressing and similar
Margarine . . . . .1 teaspoon	types . . . . .1 tablespoon
Butter . . . . .1 teaspoon	Mayonnaise . . . . .1 teaspoon

Free Choices

The following food items may be used as desired; no calories or exchanges to count.

Sugar-free diet beverages	Unsweetened gelatin
Coffee, sugar-free	Unsweetened pickles and very low-
Tea, sugar-free	carbohydrate relishes
Bouillon, fat-free	Vinegar, lemon juice, herbs and spices
Unsweetened cranberries	Lettuce, parsley and radishes

Before you can begin to eat smart or even cook smart, you must learn to shop smart. It is in the grocery store that the choices you make count the most. Putting the salt shaker away doesn't help much if the processed food in your grocery cart is heavy on sodium. If all those labels full of information are more than you can handle, this concise bit of information will make you a master shopper.

Food Packaging Terms

Low calorie...... Denotes products with no more than 40 calories per serving or 0.4 calories per gram of food.

Reduced calorie...... Must contain at least a third fewer calories than the product it replaces or resembles. Label must show a comparison between the reduced-calorie product and the standard product.

Diet...... Contains no more than 40 calories per serving. Also may have at least a third fewer calories than the product it replaces or resembles.

Lean...... On meat and poultry products, indicates no more than 10% fat by weight. The term "lean" may be used as part of a brand name with no restriction other than it must have a nutrition label.

Leaner...... Can be used on meat and poultry products that have 25% less fat than the standard product. It does not necessarily mean, however, that the product is low in fat.

Extra lean...... Denotes meat and poultry products that have no more than 5% fat by weight.

Hydrogenated fats...... Fats and oils changed from their natural liquid form to become more solid, such as most margarine and shortening. May be partially or almost completely hydrogenated. Nutritionists generally advise us to avoid completely hydrogenated oils since they resemble saturated fats. Margarines containing partially hydrogenated oils may be acceptable if they contain twice as much polyunsaturated as saturated fat.

Saturated fats...... Usually harden at room temperature and are found in animal products and some vegetable products. They tend to raise the level of cholesterol in the blood. Saturated animal fats are found primarily in beef, veal, lamb, pork, ham, butter, cream, whole milk and regular cheeses. Saturated vegetable fats are found in solid and hydrogenated shortenings, coconut oil, cocoa butter, palm oil and palm kernel oil.

No cholesterol...... May not contain cholesterol but may contain large amounts of saturated fat such as coconut or palm oil, which tend to raise the level of cholesterol in the blood.

Natural...... When referring to meat and poultry, means the product contains no artificial flavors, colors, preservatives or synthetic ingredients. No legal definition exists for the "natural" in processed foods; a natural potato chip, for example, can have artificial colors or flavors added.

Naturally flavored...... Flavoring must be from an extract, oil or other derivative of a spice, herb, root, leaf or other natural source. Naturally flavored products can also include artificial ingredients.

Organic...... No legal definition exists. Use of the term is prohibited on meat and poultry products.

Low sodium...... Limited to no more than 140 milligrams of sodium per serving.

No salt added, unsalted, without added salt...... These terms mean no salt was added during processing, but the product may still have high sodium levels due to the use of other sodium-containing ingredients such as sodium phosphate, baking powder or monosodium glutamate.

Reduced sodium...... Reduced by at least 75% from usual level of sodium per serving.

Sodium free...... Contains fewer than 5 milligrams of sodium per serving.

Very low sodium...... Contains 35 or fewer milligrams per serving.

Naturally sweetened...... Food sweetened with a fruit or juice rather than sugar. There is no regulation on this term, though, so a naturally sweetened product can contain sugar or other refined sweetener such as high-fructose corn sweetener.

Sugar free...... Does not contain sucrose (table sugar) but may contain other sweeteners such as honey, molasses or fructose, all of which add to the total calories and carbohydrates.

As you read the ingredient labels on cans and packages (more and more products are adding the information) you need to be alert. Did you know that the ingredients are listed in descending order by weight? This does not give you the actual quantity of each ingredient but it does help you identify the presence of ingredients you wish to avoid.

Reduce Fat and Cholesterol in Your Diet

Fats fall into two categories — Saturated Fat is the bad category. Cholesterol, while not strictly speaking a saturated fat, is usually included because avoiding saturated fat also avoids cholesterol. We will not attempt to explain the molecular makeup of these fats and the reasons that they should be avoided, but studies show that diets high in saturated fats and cholesterol lead to health difficulties. These fats are primarily animal fats but several vegetable fats are also saturated and therefore unhealthy. To help you identify saturated fat in your own diet or on food labels, here are some of the culprits.

Sources of Saturated Fat and Cholesterol		
bacon fat	cream	palm kernel oil
beef fat	egg and egg-yolk solids	palm oil
butter	ham fat	pork fat
chicken fat	hydrogenated vegetable oil	turkey fat
cocoa butter	lamb fat	vegetable shortening
coconut/coconut oil	lard	whole milk solids

Because meats are the major sources of saturated fats and cholesterol as well as a big part of our diets, we must learn to modify our diets in a healthy yet satisfying manner. Meat can be selected to be healthier if we just know how. The U.S. government-established meat grades are partially based on the fat content of the meat. (Prime cuts contain the most fat and marbling; Choice is leaner; Select the leanest.) Lowest fat cuts are loin, round or flank. Your butcher controls the amount of fat left on the meat for sale or processing into ground meat. Processed meats such as bologna, sausage and hot dogs can vary greatly in fat content. Check the labels.

Still another group of foods that must be considered in any good diet program are the Dairy Products. These are a special division of the animal food products and as animal products must come under the same scrutiny as meat because of the saturated fats and cholesterol. Most cheeses are made from whole milk or cream which contains butterfat (animal fat and therefore high in saturated fats and cholesterol.)

Because dairy products are also full of nutrients such as calcium that our bodies require, it is not feasible to remove them from our diets entirely. We are especially fortunate to have substitutes readily available for the most-used dairy products. Even eggs have a substitute which is made of eggs. It is the yolk of the egg that should be avoided but the white alone can be colored to resemble a whole beaten egg and used interchangeably with whole eggs in many recipes.

Try these easy modifications in your cooking:

Product	Substitution
whole milk (3½% butterfat)	low-fat milk (½, 1 or 2% buttermilk) or skim milk (0% butterfat)
cream	evaporated skim milk
whipping cream	whipped topping (check for type of oil used in preparation)
Cheddar and other ages cheeses	cheeses made from part-skim milk or reduced-fat processed cheeses
cottage cheese (cream-style)	dry curd cottage cheese or low-fat cottage cheese or ricotta cheese
sour cream	yogurt (preferably low-fat or nonfat) (see pages 11 and 91 for other ideas)
ice cream	ice milk or frozen yogurt
butter or margarine	unsaturated oils

Now about those other fats. The unsaturated fats are the good ones, but even these should be used in moderation. Most unsaturated fats are oils. Saturated fats are characteristically solid, but, as you will note from the list on page 176, some of the oils are saturated. (These oils are also used in the manufacture of soap.) Watch for the labels to specify unsaturated oils such as canola, corn, cottonseed, peanut, safflower, sunflower and sesame. Select margarine, mayonnaise, salad dressings and whipped toppings that are made with unsaturated oils.

Healthy Hints:

- Select well-trimmed meat to buy and trim it again at home to remove all visible fat.
- Limit processed meats. (This will also reduce the amount of sodium in the diet because processed meats contain salt as well as preservatives with sodium.)
- Substitute fish, chicken or turkey for red meat. (Red meats include beef and pork.)
- Remove skin and visible fat from chicken and turkey.
- Plan to use less meat by making stir-frys, casseroles and stews that are filling but use less meat per serving.
- Reduce amounts of cheese and substitute reduced-fat cheeses when possible.

Reduce Sodium in Your Diet

Sodium is present in most of the foods we eat and frequently in the water we drink. Health problems due to excessive salt in the diet include high blood pressure which can cause damage without warning or symptoms. In years past salt was used as a preservative but that is no longer necessary in this day of frozen, canned, freeze-dried, dehydrated, pasteurized and even radiated preserving methods. Unfortunately many processed foods continue to add salt in unnecessarily high amounts. We also use table salt routinely, sometimes without tasting first, and recipes call for salt in cooking when it may not be required. Taste buds may need to be trained to do without extra salt but remember that they were also trained to need it.

Sources High in Sodium	
baking powder	lemon pepper
baking soda	monosodium glutamate
bouillon	salt (sodium chloride)
brine (salt and water)	salt pork
broth	sea salt
celery salt	seasoning salt
garlic salt	self-rising flour
onion salt	soy sauce

Healthy Hints:

- Learn to use spices, herbs and other salt-free seasonings. (See pages 170 and 182.)
- Use fresh onion and garlic or onion and garlic powders rather than onion and garlic salts.
- When high-sodium ingredients such as catsup and barbecue sauce are necessary, reduce the amount or dilute with water to leave flavor but reduce the sodium.
- Use fresh ingredients rather than those convenient but often high-sodium processed foods.
- Drain the liquid and even rinse under running water to reduce the salt when you must use canned foods such as tuna and vegetables.
- Use reduced-salt substitutes whenever possible.

Reduce Sugar in Your Diet

Sugar is that enjoyable part of our diets that makes for sweet taste and almost instant energy. Even something so full of pleasure can be the source of health problems. The most obvious is diabetes, the disease resulting from the inability of the pancreas to produce enough insulin to cope with the sugar we eat. This too can be a silent disease that can cause problems without symptoms until the body is critically ill. Excessive sugar in the diet also promotes weight gain so it becomes an easy target for dieters who are, as the British say "slimming." Sugar uses many names but the results are the same.

Sources of Sugar		
brown sugar	sorghum	sucrose
fructose	corn syrup	dextrose
lactose	glucose	honey
maple sugar	molasses	invert sugar

Healthy Hints:

- Retrain your sweet tooth so that candy and other concentrated sugar foods are not so attractive.
- Substitute fresh fruits for sweets and pick up a bonus in extra fiber (see page 180).
- Use artificial sweeteners for beverages and some recipes. Be careful when using them in cooking, however, as some sweeteners lose their sweetness when heated for long periods as in baking.

DIETARY FIBER IN FOODS

Fiber is nondigestible carbohydrate which adds no calories or other nutrients to the diet. It does, however, have an important function. It absorbs water and adds bulk, making waste matter pass more quickly through the intestines. Recent studies have shown possible relationships between low-fiber diets and some diseases such as colon cancer. While no minimum daily requirement has been established, most diets can be improved by adding foods high in fiber. Fruits, vegetables and whole grains are all excellent sources of fiber.

		Amount	Weight (grams)	Fiber (grams)
BREADS	Graham cracker	2 squares	14.2	0.4
	Pumpernickel bread	¾ slice	24	1.4
	Rye bread	1 slice	25	1.7
	Whole wheat bread	1 slice	25	1.9
	Whole wheat cracker	6 crackers	19.8	2.1
	Whole wheat roll	¾ roll	21	1.5
FRUIT	Apple	½ large	83	2.1
	Apricot	2	72	1.4
	Banana	½ medium	54	1.1
	Blackberries	¾ cup	108	7.3
	Cantaloupe	1 cup	160	1.6
	Cherries	10 large	68	1.0
	Dates, dried	2	18	1.5
	Figs, dried	1 medium	20	2.2
	Grapes, green	10	50	0.6
	Grapefruit	½	87	1.1
	Honeydew	1 cup	170	1.8
	Orange	1 small	78	1.9
	Peach	1 medium	100	1.7
	Pear	½ medium	82	2.3
	Pineapple	½	78	1.2
	Plum	3 small	85	1.7
	Prunes, dried	2	15	1.4
	Raisins	1½ tbsp.	14	0.8
	Strawberries	1 cup	143	3.7
	Tangerine	1 large	101	2.0
	Watermelon	1 cup	160	0.6

		Amount	Weight (grams)	Fiber (grams)
GRAINS	All Bran	1/3 cup	28	8.5
	Bran Chex	1/2 cup	21	3.9
	Corn Bran	1/2 cup	21	4.0
	Corn Flakes	3/4 cup	21	0.4
	Grapenuts Flakes	2/3 cup	21	1.4
	Grapenuts	3 tbsp.	21	1.4
	Oatmeal	3/4 pkg.	21	2.3
	Rice, brown, cooked	1/3 cup	65	1.1
	Rice, white, cooked	1/3 cup	68	0.2
	Shredded Wheat	1 biscuit	21	2.2
	Wheaties	3/4 cup	21	2.0
MEAT, MILK, EGGS	Beef	1 ounce	28	0.0
	Cheese	3/4 ounce	21	0.0
	Chicken/Turkey	1 ounce	28	0.0
	Cold cuts/Frankfurters	1 ounce	28	0.0
	Eggs	3 large	99	0.0
	Fish	2 ounces	56	0.0
	Ice cream	1 ounce	28	0.0
	Milk	1 cup	240	0.0
	Pork	1 ounce	28	0.0
	Yogurt	5 ounces	140	0.0
VEGETABLES	Beans, green	1/2 cup	64	1.5
	Beans, string	1/2 cup	55	2.1
	Beets	1/2 cup	85	1.7
	Broccoli	1/2 cup	93	3.1
	Brussels sprouts	1/2 cup	78	3.5
	Cabbage	1/2 cup	85	2.0
	Carrots	1/2 cup	78	2.5
	Cauliflower	1/2 cup	90	2.3
	Celery	1/2 cup	60	1.0
	Cucumber	1/2 cup	70	0.8
	Eggplant	1/2 cup	100	3.4
	Lentils, cooked	1/2 cup	100	5.1
	Lettuce	1 cup	55	0.7
	Mushrooms	1/2 cup	35	0.6
	Onions	1/2 cup	58	0.9
	Potato, baked	1/2 medium	75	1.8
	Radishes	1/2 cup	58	1.3
	Spinach, fresh	1 cup	55	1.8
	Sweet potato, baked	1/2 medium	75	2.3
	Tomato	1 small	100	1.5
	Turnip greens	1/2 cup	93	2.9
	Winter squash	1/2 cup	120	3.4
	Zucchini	1/2 cup	65	0.7

NO-SALT SEASONING

Salt is an acquired taste and can be significantly reduced in the diet by learning to use herbs and spices instead. When using fresh herbs, use 3 times the amount of dried herbs. Begin with small amounts to determine your favorite tastes. A dash of fresh lemon or lime juice can also wake up your taste buds.

Herb Blends to Replace Salt

Combine all ingredients in small airtight container. Add several grains of rice to prevent caking.

No-Salt Surprise Seasoning — 2 teaspoons garlic powder and 1 teaspoon each of dried basil, oregano and dehydrated lemon juice.

Pungent Salt Substitute — 3 teaspoons dried basil, 2 teaspoons each of summer savory, celery seed, cumin seed, sage and marjoram, and 1 teaspoon lemon thyme; crush with mortar and pestle.

Spicy No-Salt Seasoning — 1 teaspoon each cloves, pepper and coriander, 2 teaspoons paprika and 1 tablespoon dried rosemary; crush with mortar and pestle.

Herb Complements

Beef — bay leaf, chives, cumin, garlic, hot pepper, marjoram, rosemary

Bread —caraway, marjoram, oregano, poppy seed, rosemary, thyme

Cheese — basil, chives, curry, dill, marjoram, oregano, parsley, sage, thyme

Fish — chives, coriander, dill, garlic, tarragon, thyme

Fruit — cinnamon, coriander, cloves, ginger, mint

Pork — coriander, cumin, garlic, ginger, hot pepper, savory, thyme

Poultry — garlic, oregano, rosemary, savory, sage

Salads — basil, chives, tarragon, parsley, sorrel

Vegetables — basil, chives, dill, tarragon, marjoram, mint, parsley, pepper

Basic Herb Butter

Combine 1 stick unsalted butter, 1 to 3 tablespoons dried herbs or twice that amount of minced fresh herbs of choice, 1/2 teaspoon lemon juice and white pepper to taste. Let stand for 1 hour or longer before using.

Basic Herb Vinegar

Heat vinegar of choice in saucepan; do not boil. Pour into bottle; add 1 or more herbs of choice and seal bottle. Let stand for 2 weeks before using.

INDEX

Microwave recipe page numbers are preceded by an M.

APPETIZERS. *See also* Dips;
    Snacks; Spreads
    Ants on a Log, 14
    Broccoli Bites, 14
    Broiled Crab Bites, 16
    Calypso Fruit Platter, 17
    Cheesy Spinach Puffs, 19
    Cold Spiced Shrimp, 19
    Eggplant Crisps, 16
    Golden Chicken Nuggets, 15
    Marinated Mushrooms, 18
    Marinated Shrimp and
        Mushrooms, 18
    Stuffed Clams, M15
    Teriyaki Meatballs, 17
    Zucchini Appetizers, 20

BARBECUE
    Barbecued Lima Beans and
        Ham, 74
    Barbecued Meat Loaf, 66
    Barbecued Pork Chops, 73
    Barbecued Pork Loin, 73
    Beef Barbecue, 56

BEEF. *See also* Ground Beef; Veal
    Beef and Broccoli Stir-Fry, 56
    Beef and Vegetable Stew, 60
    Beef Barbecue, 56
    Broiled Flank Steak, 54
    Brunswick Stew, 60
    Eye-of-Round Roast with
        Vegetables, 52
    Ginger and Orange Beef, 58
    Hearty Beef Stew, 61
    Hunan Broccoli and Beef Salad, 33
    Italian Pot Roast, M53
    Marinated Beef Tenderloin, 53
    Oven Stew, 61
    Pepper Steak, 58
    Red Flannel Hash, 57
    Sauerbraten, 59
    Simply Elegant Steak and Rice, 54
    Skillet Steak with Potatoes, 55
    Slow Cooker Beef Burgundy, 59
    Spanish Steak, 55

    Steak Cantonese, 57

BEVERAGES
    Hot Chocolate Delight, 22
    Hot Chocolate Mix, 22
    Low-Calorie Raspberry Milk
        Shake, 22
    Luscious Slush, 24
    Morning Nog, 23
    Shower Punch, 23
    Spiced Tea, 24
    Strawberry Milk Shake, 23

BISCUITS
    Quick Low-Cholesterol
        Biscuits, 142
    Whole Wheat Buttermilk
        Biscuits, 142

BREAD. *See also* Biscuits; Bread,
    Loaves; Corn Bread; Muffins;
    Pancakes
    Sesame Crackers, 143
    Whole Wheat Pita Bread, 152

BREAD, LOAVES
    Bless-Your-Heart Bread, 145
    Cracked Wheat Bread, 147
    English Muffin Loaves, 145
    Honey-Oat Bread, 146
    Sugarless Banana Bread, 144

CAKES
    Angel Food Cake, 161
    Frosted Orange Carrot Cake, 162
    Lemon Chiffon Cake, 161
    Lemon Pound Cake, 162

CHICKEN
    Baked Drumsticks, 84
    Baked Herbed Chicken, 84
    Braised Chicken Breasts, 91
    Broccoli Chicken, 92
    Brunswick Stew, 60
    California Chicken, M98
    Chicken à l'Orange, 90

Chicken and Rice Salad, 34
Chicken Breasts Veronique, 88
Chicken Cacciatore, 86
Chicken Cordon Bleu, 87
Chicken Curry, 92
Chicken Dijon, 93
Chicken Italiano, 94
Chicken Piccata, 95
Chicken Potpie, 90
Chicken Roll-Ups, M97
Chicken Scallopini, 96
Chicken Stew, 96
Chicken with Grapes, 93
Chicken with Wild Rice, 91
Crispy Herbed Chicken, 85
Crusty Baked Chicken, 86
Curried Chicken Salad, 33
Fruited Chicken Breasts, 88
Golden Chicken Nuggets, 15
Grilled Chicken Caesar Salad, 34
Inez' Crispy Baked Chicken, 85
Lago Lemon Chicken, 89
Lemon-Baked Chicken Breasts, 89
Mandarin Chicken with
    Broccoli, 95
Mushroom Dijon Chicken, 87
Orange Chicken with Lemon
    Pepper, M98
Orange-Glazed Chicken and
    Vegetables, 94
Pineapple Chicken
    (Po Lo Chi), 100
Sautéed Chicken with Apple, 99
Skinny Chicken Salad, 35
Southwestern Chicken Salad, 35
Stir-Fry Almond Chicken with
    Rice, 99
Stir-Fry Szechuan Chicken, 100
Stuffed Chicken Rolls, M97

CHILI
Three-Alarm Chili, 65
Turkey Chili, 102
Vegetable Chili, 77
Vegetarian Chili with Rice, 77

COOKIES
Apple Peanut Butter Cookies, 163
Banana Cookies, 163
Butterscotch Brownies, 164
Fresh Lemon Cookies, 165
Mudball Cookies, 165
Oatcakes, 166
Oatmeal Brownies, 164
Raisin Oat Bran Cookies, 166
Spicy Wheat Cookies, 167

CORN BREAD
Broccoli Corn Bread, 143
Mexican Corn Bread, 144

CRAB MEAT
Broiled Crab Bites, 16
Crab and Grapefruit Salad, 38
Crab Meat Puff, 114
Crab Meat Salad, 37
No-Crust Crab Meat Quiche, 115
Stir-Fry Crab Delight, 115
Tomatoes Stuffed with Crab
    Salad, 38

DESSERTS. *See also* Cakes;
    Cookies; Desserts, Frozen;
    Pies
Banana and Pineapple
    Pudding, 154
Banana Split Dessert, 155
Blackberry Cobbler, 155
Blueberry Sauce, 155
Blueberry-Grape Compote, 156
Coeur à la Crème, 167
Diet Cheesecake, 156
Granola Strawberries, 160
Maple Pears, M160
Orange Pumpkin Mousse, 159
Pavlova, 159
Spiced Apple Crisp, M154
Spiced Fruit Casserole, 158

DESSERTS, FROZEN
Frozen Raspberry Dessert, 158
Icycicles, 157
Peach Daiquiri Ice, 157
Special Ice Cream, 157

DIPS
Base for Dips, 12
Mexican Dunk, 10
Picante Sauce, 10
Relish Dip, 11

FISH. *See also* Salmon; Seafood;
    Tuna
Baked Fish Mediterranean, 106

Baked Swordfish with
    Vegetables, 112
Broiled Gingered Fish, 106
Dilled Flounder, 108
Fish Chowder, 107
Fish en Papillote, 107
Fish Paprika, 108
Orange Roughy with Lemon
    Sauce, M109
Oven-Fried Trout, 112
Poached Orange Roughy, 109
Quick and Easy Barbecued Tuna
    for One, 113
Tuna Burgers, 113

GROUND BEEF. *See also* Meat
    Loaf
Beef and Vegetable Casserole, 64
Beefy Cabbage Rolls, 62
Beefy Cabbage Wedge Meal, 63
Dolmas, 63
Lasagna Florentine, 68
Meatballs with Sauce, 65
Moussaka, 70
Pizza Casserole, 64
Potato and Ground Beef Skillet, 69
Stuffed Peppers, 70
Teriyaki Meatballs, 17
Three-Alarm Chili, 65
Zucchini Lasagna, 69

HAM
Barbecued Lima Beans and
    Ham, 74
Ham and Cheese Quiche, 74
Zesty Broccoli and Ham Salad, 36

LAMB
Easy Curried Lamb, 75
Leg of Lamb with Artichokes, 75
Spanish Lamb Stew, 76
Summer Lamb Salad, 37

LASAGNA
Lasagna Florentine, 68
Seafood Lasagna, 119
Tofu Lasagna, 80
Vegetarian Lasagna, M80
Zucchini Lasagna, 69

MEAT LOAF
Barbecued Meat Loaf, 66

Company Meat Loaf, 67
Curried Meat Loaf, 66
Oriental Meat Loaf, 67
Zesty Meat Loaf, 68

MEATLESS MAIN DISHES
Creamy Vegetable Vermicelli, 82
Herbed Spinach Pasta, 79
Light Spaghetti Primavera, 81
Pasta with Marinara Sauce, 79
Saucy Peppers on Vegetable
    Pasta, 81
Steamed Vegetables over
    Rice, 78
Tofu Lasagna, 80
Vegetable Chili, 77
Vegetarian Chili with Rice, 77
Vegetarian Lasagna, M80
Zucchini Quiche, 78

MICROWAVE
Acorn Squash with
    Cranberries, 135
Asparagus and Mushrooms, 122
California Chicken, 98
Chicken Roll-Ups, 97
Fancy Baked Potatoes, 131
Italian Pot Roast, 53
Maple Pears, 160
Orange Chicken with Lemon
    Pepper, 98
Orange Roughy with Lemon
    Sauce, 109
Salmon Steaks with Yogurt
    Sauce, 111
Seafood Stew, 120
Spaghetti Squash with
    Vegetables, 136
Spiced Apple Crisp, 154
Squash with Basil, 135
Stuffed Chicken Rolls, 97
Stuffed Clams, 15
Vegetarian Lasagna, 80

MUFFINS
Apple and Oat Bran Muffins, 147
Apple-Cinnamon-Oat Bran
    Muffins, 150
Banana Oat Muffins, 148
Banana-Oat Bran Muffins, 150
Blueberry-Oat Bran
    Muffins, 149, 150

Oat Bran Muffins, 150
Oatmeal Muffins, 151
Raisin-Oat Bran Muffins, 150
Whole Wheat Apple Muffins, 148
Whole Wheat Banana Bran
    Muffins, 149
Whole Wheat Corn Muffins, 150

NUTRITIONAL INFORMATION
Dietary Exchanges, 172–173
Dietary Fiber, 180–181
Food Packaging Terms, 174–175
Nutritional Analysis Guidelines, 8
Reduce Fat and
    Cholesterol, 176–178
Reduce Sodium, 178–179
Reduce Sugar, 179
The Well-Balanced Diet, 171

PANCAKES
Banana Pancakes, 151
Corn Bread Pancakes, 151
Healthy Pancake Mix, 152

PASTA. *See also* Lasagna; Salads,
    Pasta
Creamy Vegetable Vermicelli, 82
Herbed Spinach Pasta, 79
Light Spaghetti Primavera, 81
Pasta with Marinara Sauce, 79
Saucy Peppers on Vegetable
    Pasta, 81

PIES
Lime Pie, 168
Svelte Strawberry Pie, 168

PORK. *See also* Ham
Barbecued Pork Chops, 73
Barbecued Pork Loin, 73
Brunswick Stew, 60

POTATOES
Fancy Baked Potatoes, M131
Hashed Brown Potatoes, 132
Nacho Potato Wedges, 132
Potatoes Paprikash, 131
Scalloped Potatoes, 133

SALAD DRESSINGS
Berry Yogurt Dressing, 26
Gazpacho Dressing, 50

Honey Mustard Dressing, 50
Italian Dressing, 50
Zesty Tomato Dressing, 32

SALADS, FRUIT
Carrot Fruit Salad, 26
Chef's Fruit Salad, 26
Cranberry Salad, 27
Cranberry Waldorf Salad, 27
Fresh Fruit Salad, 28
Fruit Medley, 28
Fruit Salad Spritzer, 28
Fruited Pasta Salad, 40
Melon Basket, 29
Orange and Pear Mold, 29
Peaches and Cream Salad, 30
Pineapple and Cottage Cheese
    Mold, 30
Strawberry Fruit Mold, 31
Summer Fruit Salad, 31
Tangerine Salad, 32
Winter Fruit Salad, 32

SALADS, MAIN DISH
Chicken and Rice Salad, 34
Crab and Grapefruit Salad, 38
Crab Meat Salad, 37
Curried Chicken Salad, 33
Fruited Turkey and Seafood
    Salad, 36
Grilled Chicken Caesar Salad, 34
Hunan Broccoli and Beef
    Salad, 33
Shrimp Salad, 39
Skinny Chicken Salad, 35
Southwestern Chicken Salad, 35
Summer Lamb Salad, 37
Tomatoes Stuffed with Crab
    Salad, 38
Tuna Salad, 39
Tuna Vegetable Slaw, 40
Zesty Broccoli and Ham
    Salad, 36

SALADS, PASTA
Confetti Pasta Salad, 41
Fruited Pasta Salad, 40
Garbanzo Pasta Salad, 41
Spaghetti Salad, 43

SALADS, RICE
Crunchy Rice Salad, 42

Rice and Pea Salad, 42

SALADS, VEGETABLE
Black-Eyed Pea Salad, 44
Broccoli Salad, 45
Chilled Asparagus Salad, 44
Chinese Vegetable Salad, 49
Corn Salad, 45
Fire and Ice, 46
Herbed Potato Salad, 47
Mayan Salad, 47
Molded Gazpacho Salad, 46
Tabouli, 43
Tart and Creamy Coleslaw, 45
Tomato Aspic, 48
Wilted Spinach Salad, 48
Winter Salad with Grapes and
    Almonds, 49

SALMON
Baked Salmon Primavera, 110
Poached Salmon, 111
Salmon Loaf with Creamy Dijon
    Sauce, 110
Salmon Steaks with Yogurt
    Sauce, M111

SAUCES
Blueberry Sauce, 155
Dijon Yogurt, 127
Mexican Dunk, 10
Mock Sour Cream, 11
Picante Sauce, 10, 109
Skim Milk White Sauce, 125
Tangy Topper, 91
Yogurt Spread, 137
Yogurt-Butter Spread, 137

SEAFOOD. *See also* Crab Meat;
    Fish; Shrimp
Cajun Seafood Sauté, 119
Fruited Turkey and Seafood
    Salad, 36
Red Clam Spaghetti, 114
Scallops Saint Jacques, 116
Scallops Thermidor, 116
Seafood Lasagna, 119
Seafood Stew, M120
Stuffed Clams, M15

SHRIMP
Cold Spiced Shrimp, 19

Easy Shrimp Creole, 118
Lemon-Marinated Shrimp
    Kabobs, 117
Marinated Shrimp and
    Mushrooms, 18
Peking Shrimp, 118
Shrimp Creole over Bulgur
    Wheat, 117
Shrimp Salad, 39

SIDE DISHES
Brown Rice Pilaf, 140
Rice Supreme, 140

SNACKS
Granola, 20
Munch Mix, 21

SOUPS
Easy Egg Drop Soup, 21
Egg Drop Soup, 21
Extra-Easy Vegetable Soup, 82
Fish Chowder, 107

SOUR CREAM SUBSTITUTES
Base for Dips, 12
Mock Sour Cream, 11
Tangy Topper, 91

SPREADS
Avocado and Salmon Spread, 12
Beefy Cheese Spread, 12
Pineapple Cheese Ball, 11
Vegetable Spread, 13
Yogurt Cheese Spread, 13
Yogurt Spread, 137
Yogurt-Butter Spread, 137

SQUASH
Acorn Squash with
    Cranberries, M135
Spaghetti Squash with
    Vegetables, M136
Squash with Basil, M135
Summer Squash Casserole, 136

STEWS
Beef and Vegetable Stew, 60
Brunswick Stew, 60
Chicken Stew, 96
Hearty Beef Stew, 61
Oven Stew, 61

Seafood Stew, M120
Slow Cooker Beef Burgundy, 59
Spanish Lamb Stew, 76
Venison Stew, 76

TUNA
Tuna Salad, 39
Tuna Vegetable Slaw, 40

TURKEY
Fruited Turkey and Seafood
    Salad, 36
Roast Turkey, 101
Smoked Turkey, 101
Spinach-Filled Turkey Roll, 105
Turkey and Bean Skillet, 102
Turkey Chili, 102
Turkey Goulash, 103
Turkey Loaf, 103
Turkey Pizzas, 104
Turkey Polynesian, 104
Turkey Spaghetti Sauce, 105

VEAL
Moussaka, 70
Veal Piccata, 72
Veal Scallopini Dijon, 72
Veal-Stuffed Artichokes, 71

VEGETABLES. *See also* Potatoes;
    Squash
Asparagus and Mushrooms, M122
Baked Sweet and Sour Brussels
    Sprouts, 125
Beans and Rice, 123

Broccoli and Cheese
    Casserole, 124
Broccoli Bites, 14
Candied Sweet Potatoes, 137
Cheesy Spinach Puffs, 19
Company Carrots, 126
Eggplant Casserole, 128
Eggplant Crisps, 16
Ginger Carrots, 127
Gingered Sweet Potatoes, 138
Greek Zucchini, 139
Green Beans and Tomatoes, 124
Green Beans with Garlic, 123
Herbed Corn on the Cob, 127
Japanese Cabbage, 125
Marinated Mushrooms, 18
Marinated Shrimp and
    Mushrooms, 18
Mushrooms and Onions, 128
Okra and Tomatoes, 129
Onions Parmesan, 129
Parsnips in Orange Sauce, 130
Party Peas, 130
Pennsylvania Red Cabbage, 126
Ratatouille, 133
Snow Peas and Tomatoes, 134
Spiced Asparagus Vinaigrette, 122
Spinach Wilt, 137
Stir-Fried Snow Peas, 134
Sweet Potato and Apple
    Casserole, 138
Tomato and Corn Bake, 139
Zucchini Appetizers, 20

Venison Stew, 76

This is a perfect
gift for cooks and food lovers
for any occasion.

★★★

You may order as many of our *Answering the Call of Those in Need* cookbooks as you wish for the price of $5.00 each plus $2.00 postage and handling per book ordered. Mail to:

Tennessee Chapter #21
Telephone Pioneers of America
Room 240, Green Hills Office Building
Nashville, Tennessee 37215

Save postage and handling charges by picking up your books at the Chapter Pioneer Office, Room 240, Green Hills Office Building, Nashville, Tennessee, Telephone Number 615-665-6792.

★★★

Number books ordered _____

Amount enclosed _____

Make check payable to: Telephone Pioneers

Please Print Clearly:

NAME _____

ADDRESS_____

WORK ADDRESS _____

FLOOR OR ROOM NUMBER _____

CITY _____ STATE____ ZIP CODE_____